D1736619

REMEMBRANCE OF DAYS PAST

Glimpses of a Princely State during the Raj

REMEMBRANCE OF DAYS PAST

Glimpses of a Princely State during the Raj

JAHANARA HABIBULLAH

Translated from the Urdu by
TAHIRA NAQVI

OXFORD
UNIVERSITY PRESS

OXFORD
UNIVERSITY PRESS

Great Clarendon Street, Oxford OX2 6DP

Oxford University Press is a department of the University of Oxford.
It furthers the University's objective of excellence in research, scholarship,
and education by publishing worldwide in

Oxford New York

Athens Auckland Bangkok Bogotá Buenos Aires Calcutta
Cape Town Chennai Dar es Salaam Delhi Florence Hong Kong Istanbul
Karachi Kuala Lumpur Madrid Melbourne Mexico City Mumbai
Nairobi Paris São Paulo Shanghai Singapore Taipei Tokyo Toronto Warsaw

with associated companies in Berlin Ibadan

Oxford is a registered trade mark of Oxford University Press
in the UK and in certain other countries

© Oxford University Press 2001

ISBN 0 19 579392 7

Printed in Pakistan at
Mas Printers, Karachi.
Published by
Ameena Saiyid, Oxford University Press
5-Bangalore Town, Sharae Faisal
PO Box 13033, Karachi-75350, Pakistan.

I am dedicating my memoirs, with love
To my daughter,
Muneeza Shamsie
Who has worked so hard to help me finish this book

✛ CONTENTS ✛

✤ LIST OF PHOTOGRAPHS ✤

Between pp. 2–3

1. Nawab Najib-ud-daula.

2. General Azimuddin Khan.

3. Nawab Kalb-e-Ali Khan of Rampur.

4. Nawab Mushtaq Ali Khan of Rampur.

5. Nawab Abdus Salam Khan.

6. Sahibzada Sir Abdus Samad Khan.

7. The Prince of Wales visit, Lucknow, 1905.

8. Marble statue of Nawab Hamid Ali Khan in *durbari dress* and a diamond crown.

9. The Coronation Durbar of George V, Delhi, 1911.

10. Nawab Hamid Ali Khan's Birthday, Khasbagh Palace, Rampur.

11. Nawab Sir Amiruddin Ahmed Khan of Loharu with Hakim Ajmal Khan, Mohsinul Mulk, Delhi.

12. Moazzam Zamani Begum. She was married to Baqar Ali Khan, the adopted grandson of Mirza Ghalib.

13. Lady Abdus Samad Khan, shortly after her marriage.

✤ THANKS ✤

I cannot find words enough to thank my daughter, Muneeza and my sisters, Rafat Zamani Begum of Rampur and Begum Fakhra Masuduzzafar Khan, who have all played such an important part in encouraging me to put together these memories of mine in a book. I would also like to thank my brothers, Sahibzada Yusuf Khan and Sahibzada Yaqub Khan for their help with the historical background. I must mention my very respected and dear friend, Begum Shaista Ikramullah. Without her persuasion and encouragement I could not have accomplished this task.

My gratitude and thanks to Ameena Sayyid, the Managing Director of Oxford University Press for her interest and her patience; to my editor, Ghousia Ghofran Ali for her support; to Tahira Naqvi for translating my memoirs from the original Urdu, and to Shanul Haq Haqqi Sahib for his advice.

I also remember with affection, the pride that my late husband, Isha'at Habibullah took in the few pages I had penned during his lifetime. Of course, my thoughts have often been with my daughter, Naushaba Hasnain, who lives so far away in Canada, and has been so excited about this endeavour. I hope my grandchildren, Sa'ad and Samirah, Saman and Kamila will enjoy reading it, although to them the world that I have seen must seem but a fairy tale.

To me, the publication of this book is a dream come true and I still cannot believe it has become a reality. I apologize if there are any mistakes in my manuscript, since in my old age I ventured for the first time to pick up the pen and put whatever I had to say in view of the public.

Jahanara Habibullah
Karachi,
January 2000

❖ INTRODUCTION ❖

Begum Jahanara Habibullah was born in the princely state of Rampur in 1915. Her book, *Remembrance of Days Past* is a unique and fascinating glimpse of a fabled world. She provides a wonderful record of the customs, and pageantry to which she was an eyewitness and which now seem to belong to an Urdu *masnavi* or a distant age. These traditions remained an integral part of an Indo-Muslim culture from Mughal times until Partition and some still survive in modern India and Pakistan, under greatly changed circumstances. Furthermore, she comes from a family, which played an important part in the history of the subcontinent, for almost two hundred years. Her brief vignettes build up a collage of images that reveal the links between the old and the new.

Begum Jahanara Habibullah's Rohilla ancestors include Nawab Najib-ud-daula, who was a key figure in the eighteenth century struggle for the Mughal Empire and played a pivotal role in the decisive battle between the Afghans and the Marathas at Panipat in 1761. Her mother belonged to the literary, ruling family of Loharu, who were kinsmen of, and had very close associations with, the great Urdu poet Mirza Asadullah Khan Ghalib. Her paternal ancestors were executed by the British during the War of

Independence in 1857 and their estates were seized. The surviving family was eventually given refuge by their kinsman, the Nawab of Rampur. There they rose to high positions of state.

As Begum Jahanara Habibullah mentions in her narrative, the princes of Rampur were famous patrons of art, music and literature. They welcomed scholars and poets to their court, including Ghalib. They also preserved and nurtured the intellectual heritage of Delhi and Lucknow, both renowned cultural centres, which suffered terrible reprisals by the British, for their anti-British stance in 1857.

The British Raj became firmly entrenched in India. A growing number of Indians started to learn English, imbibe new ideas, and travel across the seas. Begum Jahanara Habibullah's great-uncle General Azimuddin Khan, the Regent of Rampur, did much to introduce modern ideas into the state, including a school for girls. This was among the many reforms that so outraged the orthodox, that it cost him his life. He was also responsible for the education and training of Begum Jahanara Habibullah's enlightened father, Sahibzada Sir Abdus Samad Khan, who became Chief Minister of Rampur and represented India in the early 1930s, at the League of Nations, the Round Table Conference and the Imperial Economic Conference in Ottawa.

Begum Jahanara Habibullah grew up in *purdah* as was the norm for women of her rank. She was taught the Quran, Urdu, and English at home. She presents a vivid portrait of the sheltered world of women, in which the great deeds of men and the events of the outside world appear merely peripheral. The living patterns in Old Delhi, described in the extract from her mother's diary had hardly changed since the eighteenth century. There were picnics in the family's mango groves near the Qutb Minar and, poetry recitals and chequer-board games with cousins, at home.

Then there is the more sumptuous world of princely Rampur, in which Begum Jahanara Habibullah grew up; her eldest sister married the future ruler, Nawab Raza Ali Khan. There is also a lively, rare, and honest account written by the Begum of Rampur herself, describing her childhood betrothal and later, her marriage. In a bridal ceremony, her lap was filled with fruits, fashioned from precious gems, for luck; she was carried in a palanquin to the palace by princes.

Begum Jahanara Habibullah gives a spellbinding account of the glittering investiture ceremony of Nawab Raza Ali Khan in 1930 at Hamid Manzil. There—amid soldiers, courtiers and processions— bejewelled elephants stood in a row and raised their trunks in salutation.

The Rampur court was known throughout India, for its brilliant cuisine too. There are descriptions of some truly inventive dishes such as pomegranate *pulao.*

Begum Jahanara Habibullah's progressive family was strongly influenced by her pioneering and liberal uncle, Dr Saiduzzafar Khan. He had helped set up the King George's Medical College in Lucknow. He had a home in Dehra Dun and it was during their stay there, that Begum Jahanara Habibullah and her sister, Begum Fakhra Masuduzzafar Khan, decided to discard *purdah.*

Remembrance of Days Past is a truly remarkable achievement for an octogenarian lady who had never written before except long, descriptive letters to her sisters. In her book, she describes her travels to Europe at the age of fifteen and subsequently, her life in cosmopolitan Mussoorie, a fashionable hill station frequented by Indian princes and the British. Then there are glimpses of her brothers and sisters including Sahibzada Mohammad Yaqub Khan who was to become a distinguished general, diplomat, and also Pakistan's Foreign Minister for nine years.

In 1942, Begum Jahanara Habibullah married Isha'at Habibullah who belonged to the feudal order, the Taluqdars of Oudh. His father Sheikh Mohammed Habibullah, Taluqdar of Saidanpur, was Vice Chancellor of Lucknow University; his mother was elected to the UP Assembly in 1937 on the Muslim League ticket and founded the party's women's wing, of which she was the first President. Her mantle passed to her daughter, Begum Tazeen Faridi, who went on to become a well-known social worker and provincial minister in Pakistan.

The timeless, traditional world that Begum Jahanara Habibullah knew vanished almost overnight at Partition. She and her husband, Isha'at Habibullah forged a new life for themselves, one which clearly belonged to a new, urban age. Isha'at Habibullah played an important role in the industrial development of Pakistan, as a professional manager and became the first Pakistani head of a multinational firm.

Begum Jahanara Habibullah's book might span a lifetime, but in terms of lifestyles and rituals it moves through centuries and is illustrated by a rare and unique collection of photographs, which provide an extraordinary record of costumes and traditions in the twentieth century.

✤ A Game of Ganjfa ✤

A few years ago, at the insistence of my sisters, Apa Jan (Her Highness the Begum of Rampur) and Bahan Fakhra (Begum Fakhra Masuduzzafar Khan), I picked up the courage to record some glimpses of my life. This endeavour has continued since 1980. While I was doing this, I was reminded of a verse by Ghalib, which likened the passing of time to the kaleidoscope of images in an old-fashioned game of cards called *ganjfa*.

محفلیں برہم کرے ہے گنجفۂ بازِ خیال
ہیں ورق گردانیِ نیرنگِ یک بتخانہ ہم

The flitting of images across the mind creates a tumult
  of impressions of assembly and dispersal
  on ceremonial occasions,
The world is indeed a game of ganjfa
  and we are but spectators of the extraordinary variety
  of a succession of magical spectacles

✦ 1 ✦

THE LINEAGE OF THE NAJIBABAD FAMILY

My father's line can be traced to the Rohilla Chieftain, Najib Khan, a Yusufzai Pathan, who received the title of Nawab Najib-ud-daula, from the Mughal Emperor, Ahmad Shah. In 1739, he travelled to India from Swabi near Swat to join his uncle, Bisharat Khan, who had already settled with a band of Pathans in Bisharatnagar, near Rampur, in the region then called Rohilkhand, lying to the east of Delhi, at the foot of the Himalayas.

He was also awarded the title of *Panj Hazari* (leader of five thousand men), in addition to a gift of property which included Nagina and Sherkot in Bijnor. Before that the *Wazir* Imad-ul-Mulk had gifted him the *Nizamat* of Saharanpur as a reward for his support in the uprising against the Mughal emperor. In 1753, the Afghan king, Ahmad Shah Abdali, who had made several incursions into India, appointed him as his plenipotentiary and he became the guardian of the new emperor, Alamgir II in 1756.

Nawab Najib-ud-daula distinguished himself as a commander in the Battle of Panipat. In recognition of his valour and leadership, Ahmad Shah Abdali awarded him the title of *Bakhsh-ul-Momlikat* (Elder of

یہ پر نواب مستطاب نجیب الدولہ بہادر و داما قبلہ سبایہ تقلم حقیر حسن علی

1. Nawab Najib-ud-daula.

2. General Azimuddin Khan.

3. Nawab Kalb-e-Ali Khan of Rampur. He invited his Najibabad kinsmen to Rampur, after they had suffered many hardships during the War of Independence, 1857.

4. Nawab Mushtaq Ali Khan of Rampur. General Azimuddin Khan protected him with his life.

5. Nawab Abdus Salam Khan.

6. Sahibzada Sir Abdus Samad Khan.

7. The Prince of Wales visit, Lucknow, 1905. The Prince of Wales (later George V) greets Nawab Hamid Ali Khan of Rampur.

8. Marble statue of Nawab Hamid Ali Khan of Rampur in *durbari* dress and a diamond crown. He is wearing an *angarkha* of heavy silk with *karchob* embroidery round the neck and the hem. The magnificent rows of pearls cover a decoration of tiny pearls on the *angarkha*. There are pearls stitched onto the shoulders in a design and also on the cuffs. The gold belt with a buckle encrusted with jewels and a pearl in the centre, is worn over a brocade *patka* which falls in folds, with golden tassels. The pearl anklets worn over his *churidar pyjama* are known as *motyon ka lacha*. A sash made of tiny pearls is linked to the jewelled scabbard and he is wearing pump shoes.

9. The Coronation Durbar of George V, Delhi, 1911. The elephant carrying Nawab Hamid Ali Khan of Rampur is right in the centre, (second from the left in the front row). Nawab Hamid Ali Khan is wearing a magnificent *kalghi* on a jewelled Rampur cap. He is seated in full regalia on a silver and gold *hawda* ornamented with the Rampur crest. The political agent is next to him. There is a *chattar* (umbrella), attached to the *hawda*. A gold work *masnad* is spread on the back of the elephant and there are cushions on either side. The

hawda is fitted on the *masnad*. The elephant's saddlecloth, is worked with floral gold embroidery, *kalabattun ka kaam*. The *mahout* in front is wearing a red uniform. He is holding a *chanwar* (a fly swat with a gold handle), and an *an kus* (a gold rod), to control the elephant. The elephant is caparisoned with gold jewellery, including *goshwaras* hanging from both his ears, a net over his head with a big gold ornament, resembling a *teeka* on his forehead. There is a gold bar at the bottom of the saddlecloth, with two elephant boys walking alongside.

10. Nawab Hamid Ali Khan's birthday, Khasbagh Palace, Rampur. Second row, extreme right: Sahibzada Sir Abdus Samad Khan, second row, extreme right. Front row from L to R: Nawabzada Jaffer Ali Khan, Nawab Sir Amiruddin Ahmed Khan of Loharu, Maharajah of Bikaner, Nawab Hamid Ali Khan of Rampur, Nawab of Palanpur, Nawabzada Raza Ali Khan (later Nawab of Rampur), Nawabzada Abdul Karim Khan. Right at the back are two uniformed palace *khidmatgars*. One, on the right is Ram Prashad, who had witnessed the assassination of General Azimuddin Khan.

11. Nawab Sir Amiruddin Ahmed Khan of Loharu with Hakim Ajmal Khan, Mohsinul Mulk. Delhi, 1912. The Nawab is draped in a handsome *choga*, worn in Central Asia by the Mughals; it is embroidered with *zari* work and has a gold braiding to give it a finish. He is also wearing a *churidar pyjama*, boots and a velvet Loharu cap with gold work. Hakim Ajmal Khan is in an *angharkha* and a cap of Persian lamb.

12. Moazzam Zamani Begum. She was married to Baqar Ali Khan, the adopted grandson of Mirza Ghalib. She died in 1945 at the age of 93 and is seen here with her great-great-grandson, Parvez Mirza, the present Nawab Allauddin Ahmed Khan of Loharu.

13. Lady Abdus Samad Khan in a *farshi pyjama*, shortly after her marriage.

the Kingdom), *Amir-ul-Umara* (Chief among the Nobles). He was given the responsibility of protecting and governing of the Mughal Empire as virtual vice-regent. The title of Nawab was also bestowed on other members of Nawab Najib-ud-daula's family. This was an honorary title which was inherited by my grandfather.

Nawab Jalaluddin Khan was the last ruler of Najibabad. His predecessor, who was also his brother, supported the Mughal emperor, Bahadur Shah Zafar in the War of Independence 1857 against the British. They wreaked terrible destruction on the entire family. Nawab Jalaluddin Khan and his brother-in-law, Nawab Sa'adullah Khan, were both executed after a court martial and their land seized, although they were innocent of any complicity in the uprising. Nawab Sa'adullah Khan was my great-grandfather.

My family suffered many hardships until Nawab Kalb-e-Ali Khan, became the ruler of Rampur and gave them shelter. My family was closely linked to the ruling families of Rampur and Loharu. Nawab Jalaluddin Khan had married into the Nawab of Rampur's family, twice. His first wife, Majlis Ara Begum, gave birth to a daughter, Shamsunnissa Begum, who married Nawab Alauddin Ahmad Khan, the ruler of Loharu. After Majlis Ara Begum died, his second wife, Qudsia Begum bore four children, including General Sahibzada Azimuddin Khan.

❖ ❖ ❖

GENERAL AZIMUDDIN KHAN

He fell victim to a court intrigue in Rampur and was assassinated in 1891.

There is no doubt that General Azimuddin Khan was one of our family's most eminent personalities. A man of outstanding intellect, with a commanding personality, he sacrificed his life for truth and loyalty. He was also a patrician who took care of all his relatives.

General Azimuddin Khan was my father's uncle; Apa Jan's mother, was his daughter. I have had occasion to go through Sahibzada Irshadullah Khan's book[1] and I quote some of the events mentioned there:

General Azimuddin Khan was Nawab Najib-ud-daula's great-great-grandson. He was born in Najibabad, three years before the War of Independence 1857. After Nawab Jalaluddin Khan and Nawab Sa'adullah Khan were both sentenced to death by the British, it was later discovered that they were innocent of any wrongdoing. The British government gave their widows and their children an allowance. In circumstances of great hardship this family travelled to Moradabad and Azimuddin Khan received his early schooling at Moradabad.

At that time, Nawab Kalb-e-Ali Khan was the ruler of Rampur. During his reign, Azimuddin Khan's uncle, General Ali Asghar Khan, was the commander of the Rampur forces. He sent for Azimuddin Khan, who subsequently received his training in the army. He became an accomplished sportsman, taught by some of the best known instructors in Hindustan. He was adept at riding, swimming, spear-hunting and target-shooting, and his fame as a huntsman spread far and wide. Nawab Kalb-e-Ali Khan greatly admired him, as a role model and trusted him implicitly. Towards the end of his reign, the Nawab appointed him as his plenipotentiary and representative to liaison with the British.

The Nawab had such confidence in him, that on his deathbed he placed the hand of his son and heir, Mushtaq Ali Khan, in General Azimuddin Khan's hand and gave instructions about his accession. He asked the General to ensure that Mushtaq Ali Khan, who was mildly paralyzed, would not be impeded from becoming Rampur's ruler, on account of his handicap. The General discharged these duties impeccably. He also employed tutors to teach the young prince English and sent for a doctor from England who helped the Nawab overcome much of his difficulty. This excited the jealousy of Nawab Mushtaq Ali Khan's half-brother, Haider Ali Khan. He became the centre of an intrigue against the General, who had to contend with many plots to overthrow him.

In 1887, Nawab Mushtaq Ali Khan ascended the throne. His first action was to appoint the General as his Chief Minister. But his reign was very short. He passed away in 1889 and his son, Nawab Hamid Ali Khan, who was only fourteen, succeeded him. As he was still a minor, a Council of Regency was formed, with Sir Auckland Colvin, the Governor of the UP and the General, as its trustees.

The General conducted the affairs of Rampur with efficiency and diligence. He virtually ruled Rampur for four years and introduced many reforms. He opened English and Urdu medium schools for boys; and in domestic skills for girls. He set up a modern hospital run by a qualified doctor and also a traditional *shifa khana* run by a *hakim*. He built new roads, bridges, canals, dams and irrigation systems, and laid great emphasis on law and order.

As a result of these salutary reforms, a *maulvi* sahib issued a *fatwa*, denouncing these changes as violations of the *shariah*. Some of the Rampur Pathans opposed English education. Another faction was led by Haider Ali Khan, who resented the General. These three groups conspired to assassinate him. He was invited to a wedding and since it was summer he was wearing only a light cotton *angarkha* (otherwise he always wore a bullet proof vest). After the celebrations, he was heading home in his phaeton. As he crossed a narrow street, the killers sprayed him with bullets. Even when he had been severely wounded, he addressed the killers boldly and courageously, saying 'I have recognized you!' Stumbling a few steps, along a wall, he finally fell down unconscious and died, shortly thereafter. The news of his death shocked the people of Rampur and devastated his family. How sad that this great man was cut down in the prime of life, by a malevolent, murderous attack!

مرثیہ جرنیل عظیم الدین خاں مرحوم ۱۸۹۱ء

از: مولانا شبلی نعمانی

بطورِ یادگار ایک مرثیہ پیش کرتی ہوں

تا کے ز غمِ نہاں نہ گویم   گویند مگو چہ جاں نہ گویم

دارم جگرو می توانم   کافسانہ بہ داستاں نہ گویم

از عربدۂ فلک نہ نالم   از نیک و بدِ جہاں نہ گویم

از نالۂ دل اثر نخواہم   از دارمِ جگر نشاں نہ گویم

رفت آنچہ ز دورِ چرخ بر من   یک حرف ازاں میاں نہ گویم

این جملہ ہمی توانم اما   نتواں کہ این داستان نہ گویم

در ماتمِ خانِ اعظم الدین   جو قصہ خوں چکاں نہ گویم

آہ از غمِ این چنیں امیرے

شیرِ انگن و شیرِ شیرگیرے

Marsia
Dedicated to General Azimuddin Khan (d. 1891)
by Maulana Shibli Naumani

I

How long can I remain silent about my secret grief?
People enjoin silence, but how long should I refrain from
*   expressing my grief?*

My heart is so full that I cannot bear
To allow the tale of those events to remain unrelated.

It's possible I forego the tale of cruelty meted out by the
*   heavens*
And say nothing about the trials and tribulations of this
*   world*

And that I don't accept the effects of my heart's pain
And mention not the grief that has scarred my soul.

Whatever tyranny life has dealt me,
I utter not a single word about it.

All this I will do gladly, but
I cannot desist from telling this tale of woe,

And lamenting the passing of Khan-e-Azamuddin
I cannot remain silent about the bloody tale of his death,

The tale of an Amir who was one
Who hunted lions, trapped lions, and was a lion himself.

چوں زین غمِ جانگداز گریم
گریم صد بار و باز گریم

درخاک شدن امیرِ زیبا
یا تہمتن اوفتادہ در چاہ

مہماں یکے بہ شب شدو خاست
تا باز رود سوئے بنگاہ

کم حوصلہ گانِ سفلہ چند
بودند نشستہ در کمین گاہ

کابکہ چوں درمقابل آمد
آن گبرو شاں دول بہ ناگاہ

یکجا بر و کشاد دادند
شش تیرو یکے نشانہ شدآہ

برجبۂ صبر چیں نیفگند
با آن ہمہ زخمہائے جانکاہ

برخاک فتاد و باز برخاست
پس طے نمود پارۂ راہ

آسودے براہ وزان پس
افسانہ عمر گشت کوتاہ

باصد سخنے بماند خاموش
آں گجر بیارِ میدازِ جوشں

II

When I weep in lamentation for him
I weep a hundred times and still I want to weep.

That great Amir has fallen to the earth
Like Rustum falling into a well.

One day he was a guest at someone's house,
He rose to leave to go home,

On the way some dastardly knaves
Lay low in hiding,

And when his carriage drove up
Those tyrants suddenly

Made him a target and
Shot six bullets that hit their mark.

Even with these deadly wounds
Not a frown appeared on his patient brow.

Falling to the ground, he rose again,
Travelled a short distance,

Stopping awhile once along the way,
And then ended the story of his life.

He, who had a thousand things to say
Was silenced,

Like a turbulent ocean
Finally at peace.

❖ ❖ ❖

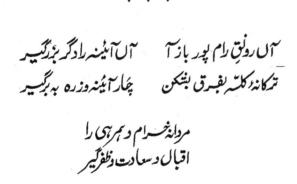

Return, you who have left us,
Revive the brightness of Rampur, its glory,

Place upon your head the crown of the courageous Turks,
Carry the armour in your hands,

Come with a manly stride
Bringing with you good fortune, generosity, and victory.

❖ ❖ ❖

MY GRANDFATHER
NAWAB ABDUS SALAM KHAN

I remember my grandfather, Nawab Abdus Salam Khan, well. He had a very dignified and impressive personality. He was well-versed in English, Arabic, and Persian, and he authored *Sarguzasth-e-Nawab Najib-ud-daula*, a book about his ancestor. He loved reading. He had put together a large collection of rare and valuable books in his library. After his death, this was presented as a gift to the Aligarh Muslim University, by his sons. God blessed him with three children including my father, Sahibzada Abdus Samad Khan.

❖ ❖ ❖

MY FATHER
SAHIBZADA SIR ABDUS SAMAD KHAN

Papa was born in Moradabad in 1874. He went to school in Lucknow and came home to Rampur for his holidays. At the time, Nawab Hamid Ali Khan was very young and the British had set up a Council of.Regency. General Azimuddin Khan who was in charge of his education, consulted my grandfather and suggested that since Papa and the Nawab were the same age, they should be educated together. The Governor of the UP agreed to this and his nephew, Captain Colvin, was their tutor. They had English, Urdu, Persian, and Arabic tutors too and the standards they demanded were very high. This education, widened Papa's horizons and he developed a broad vision. One of the tutors, Mr Bidden, used to call him 'MacDuff'. This became his nickname.

In 1893, at the age of eighteen, Papa accompanied Nawab Hamid Ali Khan on a world tour, which is recorded in a book *Seher-e-Hamidiya*.[2] They went to

China, Japan, America, Europe and came home, accompanied by two English tutors, a Persian tutor, several secretaries, cooks, *khidmatgars* and Thomas Cook's huge staff.

Nawab Hamid Ali Khan assumed the reigns of government at the age of twenty-one. For a short while Papa continued as his companion and aide, but soon became the Chief Minister. He was entrusted with the care and management of the affairs of state—a role he fulfilled for thirty years—without interference from the Nawab in any of the official business. Papa executed his duties with the utmost care and diligence. He was closely associated with the political department, the governor and the viceroy, and had a large circle of friends, including several rulers, particularly the Maharajah of Bikaner, the Maharajah of Jaipur, the Maharajah of Kashmir, and the Nizam of Hyderabad.

On one occasion, the Nizam of Hyderabad visited Rampur. He was very taken by the grandeur and lifestyle of the royal house. He turned to Papa and exclaimed 'All that I have heard about Rampur was true! I have seen it today with my own eyes.' It is said that the Nizam liked a gold *hukkah* so much, that it was presented to him as a gift.

In 1930, Nawab Hamid Ali Khan passed away. His death came as a shock to everyone in Rampur, especially Papa, who felt the loss of his old friend, deeply. Some time later, the investiture of Nawab Raza Ali Khan and Apa Jan, his Begum, were held at Hamid Manzil in the Fort, accompanied by grand celebrations. Apa Jan was given the official title of Her Highness Rafat Zamani Begum of Rampur.

In 1931, Papa attended the Round Table Conference in London, as a representative of the Indian princely states, and met King George V at the royal reception. In 1932, he attended the second

Round Table Conference and left for Ottawa in July as a member of the Indian delegation to the Imperial Economic Conference. The following year, he was invited to the League of Nations in Geneva to represent India and was knighted in 1934. He also accompanied the Nawab and Begum of Rampur on a voyage to Europe; in London they were received in audience by King George and Queen Mary. Afterwards, he travelled independently to Europe and was present at the English court for the coronation of King George VI and Queen Elizabeth. In 1937, he left for Kashmir, where he had been appointed Home Minister.

Papa was in Srinagar for four years. With the outbreak of the Second World War in 1939, everything changed. Papa thought it best we return to Rampur. My youngest brother, Yaqub was in the army. He received orders to leave for the Saharan front. After a year and a half of active service, which included the siege of Tobruk, he was taken prisoner in May 1942, during Rommel's advance on El-Alamein in Egypt. This caused great concern to us all. After a long period of waiting, during which we suffered tremendous anxiety, we heard that Yaqub was in a German POW camp. This news proved especially distressing for my father, who was already ailing.

NOTES

1. Irshadullah Khan, (Retd.) Home Minister, Riyasat Rampur, *Halaat Khandaan Maulvi Ghulam Gilani Khan Sahib Marhoom Rampur*, Published Privately, Rampur, November 1955.
2. Maulvi Farrukhi, *Seher-e-Hamidiya: Roznama Siyahat Aley Hazrat Nawab Mohammed Hamid Ali Khan Sahib Bahadur*, published by Mohammed Qadir Ali Khan Sufi, Agra, undated.

✥ 2 ✥

THE LINEAGE OF THE LOHARU FAMILY

My mother's ancestors belonged to the family of
Khwaja Yusuf Beg, whose shrine and library can still
be found in Bokhara. During the reign of the Mughal
Emperor, Shah Alam, three of the brothers, Mirza Arif
Beg, Mirza Alam Beg, and Mirza Qasim Beg came to
Hindustan. They were associated with the Mughal
Qabila-e-Barlas and were related to the Wazir of
Bokhara.

In Hindustan, they made a name for themselves by
performing heroically in the wars. In 1804, Lord Lake
awarded Nawab Ahmad Bakhsh Khan, the principality
of Firozepur and the Raja of Alwar gave him Loharu.
Nawab Ahmad Bakhsh Khan, was my mother's great-
grandfather. Her family maintained residence in Gali
Qasim Jan, the street in Delhi that had been named
after Mirza Qasim Beg, the ancestor of the Loharu
family; it was here that Urdu's greatest poet, Mirza
Asadullah Khan Ghalib had also lived.

Delhi

This was the fabled capital of Hindustan, which was almost completely destroyed by the War of Independence 1857. But the golden rays of history shed a new light on Delhi again and it became the centre of the arts, learning, and culture once more. The literary traditions of Delhi, its citizenry, its poetry, its culture and manners were all associated with Old Delhi. It was Ghalib who gave *Urdu-e-Mualla*, the Urdu language, a new brilliance and Urdu replaced Persian as the literary language of northern India. Ghalib brought to Urdu poetry, a philosophic depth, a refinement and lustre that has continued to distinguish it to this day.

How well Mir Taqi Mir puts it:

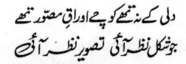

These were not the streets of Delhi, these were the strokes of an artist's brush,
Each image assumed a supernatural beauty.

❖ ❖ ❖

MIRZA ASADULLAH KHAN GHALIB
(1797–1869)

The Loharu family had a long and intimate association with Mirza Ghalib. He was married to Umrao Begum; she was the daughter of Nawab Ilahi Bakhsh Khan Ma'ruf and a niece of Ahmad Bakhsh Khan, the ruler of Loharu. Thus, Ghalib became a son-in-law of the Loharu family.

None of Mirza Ghalib's children survived, so he adopted his wife's nephew, Mirza Zainul Abidin Arif. Unfortunately, Zainul Abidin died at an early age, a tragedy that left Mirza Ghalib in deep and abiding distress. He wrote a moving *noha* which is considered to be a masterpiece. After the death of his adopted son, Mirza Ghalib raised his two infant sons. One of them, Baqar Ali Khan Kamil, was my great-grandfather. He was married to Nawabzadi Moazzam Zamani Begum, alias Bigga Begum. She was the daughter of Nawab Ziauddin Ahmad Khan of Loharu.

We all called her Nani Amma. I remember her as a very old, wrinkled and fair-skinned lady, with a strong personality. Having lived in the Ghalib household, she had observed Mirza Ghalib at very close quarters and had often heard him recite his verses. Here's a story related by my grandmother and passed on to us by Ammajan, my mother.

One evening, Mirza Ghalib came home and said to his wife 'Look, how beautiful the weather is, my dear. There is such an enchanting breeze blowing. This romantic setting finds you and I alone, except for our daughter-in-law whose presence is such a speck in the eye, such an intrusion.' Mirza Ghalib's wife began to upbraid him for making these improper remarks and poor Nani Amma doubled with embarrassment and shyly sought refuge in the small verandah outside.

Nani Amma had three daughters. Her second, was my grandmother, Sahibzadi Fatima Sultan Begum. She was married to Nawabzada Bashiruddin Ahmad Khan, the son of Nawab Alauddin Ahmad Khan, the ruler of Loharu and Sahibzadi Shams-un-Nissa Begum of Najibabad.

Nawab Alauddin Ahmad Khan wrote poetry under the pen-name, 'Alai'. He was a close friend of Mirza Ghalib, and his favourite pupil, and had been named as his literary heir. Mirza Ghalib regarded Alai with such affection that at Alai's request, he wrote a moving *ghazal*. Several of its verses reflect the recurrent romantic theme of pain and suffering that gave Mirza Ghalib's lyrics a charged meloncholy, in which human and devotional love were inseparable. The *ghazal* was dedicated to Alai with the words:

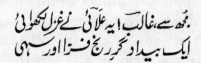

At Alai's insistence I wrote this ghazal, Ghalib,
Yet another ode of sorrow and distress.

❖ ❖ ❖

MY MOTHER
SAHIBZADI ALIYA SULTAN BEGUM

In 1888, a daughter was born in the *mahalsera* of Nawabzada Bashiruddin Mirza of Loharu in Gali Qasim Jan. The infant girl was taken over by her *Khala*. She raised her with special love and care, in the midst of the culture and traditions of Old Delhi. She was named Aliya Sultan Begum, and she grew up to become my mother, Ammajan. She was married to Sahibzada Abdus Samad Khan, a nobleman of Najibabad, and after her marriage had the occasion to observe first hand, the glory and splendour of the royal house of Rampur.

Life in the Mahalsera

Hectic activities enlivened the *zenana* in the *mahalsera* at Gali Qasim Jan with frequent gatherings of writers, aristocrats, relatives and friends; it was spacious enough to provide a separate suite of rooms for each family living there. In the *dalaan*, which faced a central courtyard, there were seating arrangements with white bolsters and cushions, scattered across white *masnads* for sitting. These were spread on *chandni*; at meal times, *dastarkhans* were laid out on the *chandni* too. All the relatives ate together, since there was no *purdah* from the men in the family, especially cousins and uncles.

Some of the activities the young people engaged in included *bai'at baazi*, a poetry game, or *pacheesi* and *chausar*, which are different types of chequer-board games using pawns. On other occasions there would be someone playing the *harmonium* or singing a *ghazal*. There were frequent literary discussions, or *mushairas*. The leading light among the women was Ammajan's literary cousin, Hamida Sultan Begum. She recalls that the following verse by Ammajan's close relative, the poet Sa'il, for example, drew much applause:

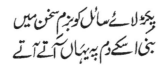

Sa'il, was persuaded to attend the symposium,
But was prey to inexpressible tension and nervousness at
composing suitable verses on his way.

While this was going on, the *begumaat* were always preparing for some wedding or the other. From the time a child was born, to his or her wedding, there was always some ritual or ceremony that demanded attention. In addition to these tasks, there were religious offerings such as *nazr*, *niaz*, *koonday* on specific occasions, or there would be a *mi'laad*, to celebrate the birth of the Prophet (PBUH), or the observance of *Muharram*.

An Excerpt From Ammajan's Diary

'I was born three years after my parents made devotional prayers at the shrine of Khwaja Moinuddin Chishti. My Khala, who had no children, adopted me, cherished me and loved me dearly; Nani Amma's *mughalani* and *darogha* looked after me. When I was four years old my *Bismillah* ceremony was celebrated and it was then that a teacher was appointed for my education. After I had completed the Quran with my *ustani*, a *maulvi sahib* was appointed to teach me Urdu and Persian, but I remained hidden from him, behind a curtain.

'As soon as the rainy season began, swings were put up for us. Sometimes we would all go to the Qutb Sahib.[1] We would leave home very early in the morning and arrive at the Qutb by midday. We would spend the night at our house there and then wander around the Qutb the following day. Ammrian and Shamsi Talaab[2] were also places that we visited.

'Since the olden days, there had been an annual *urs* at Qutb Sahib. The *charioun ka mela*[3] there drew heavy crowds. Our house was a double-storied building, so that we could easily watch the *mela* from the upstairs balcony. The weather here was lovely during the rainy season and we had also heard that in olden times, the king, accompanied by his *begumaat* and his entourage, would stay at Qutb Sahib for four months at a time. In Noor Bagh[4] the trees were laden with mangoes, ready for the picking and were surrounded by lush greenery. A feast would be prepared in the shade of the trees, under gathering clouds and a light drizzle, while the *koel* sang in the branches. Together with our young friends, we would swing and sing *malhar*[5]:

14. The Governess, Mrs Berry with Fakhra.

15. Fakhra and Jahanara. Fakhra (L) wears a cap and *sarasari teeka* on her forehead. A *hansli* falls over her large English bib. Her *kurta pyjama* is embroidered at the edges. Jahanara (R) is in an English bonnet and dress.

16. From L to R. Fakhra, Yusuf, Jahanara. It was the custom to dress up little girls in *achkans*, that the two sisters are wearing, with tight *churidar pyjamas* and English boots. Fakhra is wearing anklets called *chahgals*. Their glittering caps, were embellished with *go'ta* and were also the fashion. Their baby brother is dressed up in English clothes and a bonnet.

17. Askari Begum (later Rafat Zamani Begum of Rampur) and Nawabzada Raza Ali Khan, the *Waliahed* of Rampur at their *nikah*, 1907. He is wearing a heavily embroidered cap of gold *karchob* and is in an *angarkha* with a silk floral design. She is wearing a *farshi pyjama* and a *dupatta* decorated with *go'ta* and *kiran*.

18. Rafat Zamani Begum in a *farshi pyjama*. She is wearing a *sarasari teeka* on her head.

جھولا کن ڈارو سے امریاں

دو سکھی جھولیں ۔ دو ہی جھولادیں

چاروں ملکیاں مہبول بھلیاں

Who are these four maids,
Swinging fairy-like through the air?
Creating a riot of colour
Their many splendoured costumes
Mingling with the tints of flowering trees
To form a moving tableau
Of loveliness

— Amir Khusro

❖ ❖ ❖

AMMAJAN'S ARRIVAL IN RAMPUR
1914

After their marriage, my father entrusted the care and
upkeep of the *zenana* in his Rampur house, Rosaville,
to Ammajan. There, she saw around her a new
environment, strangers who became in-laws, a new way
of life, a large mansion, and scores of servants. In
these difficult circumstances, she mastered the art of
housekeeping with great skill. Her in-laws gave her
the title of *Ameer Dulhan.*

Ammajan was a good-natured, simple, and religious
person. She was a great letter writer and had a very
beautiful hand. She was neat and orderly, had good
taste, knew all the rules of etiquette and was talented
too. She did embroidery with such skill and artistry
that not a single knot could be seen. The desserts she
made were extraordinary, especially sweets known as
gosh-e-feel, which were pinched and shaped to resemble
an elephant's ears and were steeped in syrup.

Ammajan was blessed with children as well as rank and status. In 1932, she travelled all over England and Europe. She mentioned three things about Europe that impressed her the most: namely respect for women, respect for law, and respect for time. The best part of her personality was her simplicity, a quality that endeared her to everyone.

The Loharu family and that of Syed Muratab Ali in Lahore, had a long-standing friendship. The first time I heard Lady Muratab Ali refer to my mother as Aliya Begum, I was astonished—I had never heard anyone call Ammajan by her proper name before! Lady Muratab Ali's son, Syed Babar Ali became a good family friend. He has told me that Papa was often mentioned in his home, with great regard as 'Chief Sahib', a name used for him by everyone in Rampur.

Ammajan performed Hajj after Partition. The last years of her life were spent in worship and the recitation of the Quran. I lost my beloved mother in February 1967.

جاتے ہوتے ہتے ہو قیامت کو ملیں گے

کیسا خوب قیامت کا ہے گویا کوئی دن اور

At your departure you say 'We'll meet on the calamitous day of resurrection,'
Well said indeed—is there another such day.

– Ghalib

NOTES

1. The popular name for the verdant area surrounding the Qutb Minar and the shrine of Hazrat Bakhtiar Kaki.
2. Ammrian was a mango grove on a little hillock and Shamsi Talaab was a pond. Both were places of great beauty and popular as picnic spots.
3. A funfair named after the wooden poles and sticks decorated with garlands and flowers and carried in a procession.
4. An orchard belonging to Ammajan's family.
5. Amir Khusro's romantic songs about the rainy season.

✤ 3 ✤

MY BROTHERS AND SISTERS

My eldest sister was called Askari Begum, but afterwards, her father-in-law, Nawab Hamid Ali Khan, the ruler of Rampur, gave her the name of Rafat Zamani Begum. Her mother, Nadir Zamani Begum, who was the daughter of General Azimuddin Khan, died very young. After that, Papa married Ammajan. Their children were: Fakhra, Jahanara, Yusuf, Yunus, and Yaqub. We called our eldest sister, Apa Jan. We were all raised with great love and affection and, brought up in the same house and in the same environment. I was very mischievous as a child. I constantly twittered like a myna bird and was everyone's favourite. Apa Jan was particularly fond of me and I was with her most of the time. Her governess, Mrs Berry, liked to dress me up in English clothes that made me look like a doll. At the time of Apa Jan's wedding, I was five years old.

✤ ✤ ✤

APA JAN'S WEDDING

Apa Jan was married in 1920, with great pomp and ceremony, to the *Waliahed* of Rampur, Nawabzada Syed Raza Ali Khan. Their *nikah* had taken place when she was only five and he was six.

I remember it was winter when she got married. There was a big gathering of guests in the verandahs of the *zenana*. Apa Jan remained in a central room, in accordance with the rituals of the *manjha* ceremony. After her *rukhsati*, when she left for her new home, we were separated, but the strange part of it is, that the bond we had shared in childhood, remained with us for ever.

The following is an account of her *nikah* and wedding[1] in her own words:

'The date was 24 March 1912 and I was five years old. The *zenana* at Rosaville was full of the *begumaat* from the Royal Fort. In their midst, I sat in my grandmother's lap, on a golden *masnad*. I was wearing a *karchobi* suit and had a small *teeka*, on my forehead; my grandmother supported my large *nath*, with her hand.

'The celebrations, consisting of dancing and singing were in full swing. The wedding songs began. My mother-in-law and sisters-in-law said *Bismillah*, and tied the *imam zamin* on my right arm and slipped silver and gold bands along with a jewel-studded ring on my finger. A gold-trimmed handkerchief was placed in my lap. First the married women covered their heads and placed a coconut in my lap and then filled my lap with dried nuts and fruit. All these were made of gold and studded with precious stones.

'Outside, in the *mardana*, the Sunni *Qazi* Sahib of the city and the Shia *mujtahid* performed the *nikah* ceremony. Because my father was Hanafi and my father-in-law was Asna-Ashri, the *nikah* was performed according to the tenets of both sects. Immediately afterwards, the *zenana* inside was filled with tumultous celebrations.

'The earliest stories of my childhood have been passed on to me by my grandmother, Dadimayya, because I was too young to remember anything. However, I do remember events that occurred when I was eight years old. I was told that I bowed low and raising my hand to my forehead, offered *salaams* to everyone and then came outside with my wet nurse. Nawab Hamid Ali Khan, whom I called Nana Huzoor, said, "Daughter Askari, hold out your hands," and when I did, he emptied a bagful of pearls into my cupped palms. Thinking of it as a game, I separated my hands and the pearls spilled on the carpet. When he saw this, Nana Huzoor burst into laughter. I don't remember exactly what he said, but his words were to the effect: "Sweet flower-like bride, may you always smile like this."

'After the ceremonies, my father-in-law said to my father, "Abban Mian[2] from now on she represents Our Honour. We will entrust her to your care for a while. She will have a guard, and a horse drawn carriage will come from Our stables to take her for a drive. In the summer, We will arrange for the family to accompany Askari to Nainital."

'This is how time passed. I always returned to Rampur on the 29th of August because it was important for me to attend the *zenana durbar* on 31 August, the occasion of Nawab Hamid Ali Khan's birthday. My gift of homage would be presented to him after my mother-in-law had presented hers.

'It is necessary to explain that since childhood, my husband and myself were good friends and played together as any young brother and sister would. One day, my husband, the *Waliahed*, Nawabzada Raza Ali Khan, said angrily to His Highness "Abba Sahib, Askari is always dressed in a frock and a hat. How can she become my bride? How will she wear a veil?"

'He replied, lovingly, "Nabboo Sahib[3], *Inshallah* when We bring Our beautiful granddaughter home after the wedding, dressed up as a lovely bride, the whole world will gasp in wonder and you too will be happy to see her."

'At the age of nine or ten we both developed a sort of reticence when we were together. We would sit in the presence of Nawab Hamid Ali Khan, but until he addressed us we didn't utter a word. Gradually we began to be uncomfortable in each other's company.

'Suddenly, in the beginning of 1920, Nana Huzoor told my father that the children were now both grown up and my *rukhsati* should take place formally. My father said, "Sir, the young man is only fourteen and has not even completed his education. As for the girl, she has been raised without any formal experience of court life. If you permit, can we wait a while longer?" But my father-in-law stubbornly insisted on having the *rukhsati* right away. This sort of exchange continued for some time and relations between the two became somewhat strained. Finally, on 4 November 1920, Nana Huzoor arrived with the whole family and the ceremonies that usually take days to be completed, were performed in minutes.

'... at the time of the *rukhsati*, a lady carried me into a palanquin and closed all the curtains. At this moment, there was a loud rolling of the drum and a *shehnai* started playing the *raag*. Then two heralds announced His Highness's lineage and described all the battles his ancestors had fought and won.

The language was very old and difficult to follow, for it was neither Urdu nor Hindi. All you knew was that it was a eulogy of the Royal Family.

'My beloved Nana Huzoor called out, "Brothers, I give shoulder to this palanquin. Come and join me." All the men of his family, picked it up and walked with it, from Rosaville to Khasbagh Palace. Guns resounded from the palace grounds to tell the whole of Rampur "The palanquin of His Highness's daughter-in-law has left her home."

'The bridegroom rode in a *havadar*. *Khazanchis* dressed in *angarkhas* and special caps, carried trays full of silver and gold coins to my father-in-law. He gathered them up in fistfuls and scattered them over the palanquin, *en route*, until we arrived at Khasbagh Palace. When the procession reached the *deohri* of Shahenshah Manzil (which is now called Rafat Mahal) the men left and the ladies came forward to take me to the *mehfil khana*. Inside, the court singers, Haideri Jan and Bigga Jan sang a song of congratulations, a *mubarakbadi*, in their purest tones.'

❖ ❖ ❖

THE RAINY SEASON AND
SAWANI CELEBRATIONS

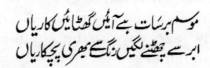

It is the rainy season, black clouds gather,
From the clouds come sprinkles of colourful water.

During our childhood, the rainy season, in the months of *Sawan* and *Bhadun*, meant excitement and fun. The clouds gathered thickly, lightening flashed, thunder rolled and the constant '*Cuhoo! Cuhoo!*' of the *koel* was heard. The branches of the mango trees swayed. Thick, green foliage wore a cleansed, fresh look, the flowers were bursting with colour so bright that one would think they had been hand-painted. There was greenery everywhere. Special snacks were ceremoniously prepared. As for us young girls, our thoughts turned immediately to the *jhoola*, the swing. We gathered all our friends, wearing bright, *chunree dupattas* and light green bangles. What beautiful multi-coloured designs those tie-and-dye *chunrees* used to have: *dhanak*, *lehria*, *aabe-e-lehr* and *bandhini*. The minute the raindrops started falling we ran to the swings. A silken cord would be attached to the *hindola*, the wooden frame of the swing, to support a colourful, hand painted plank. We would swing high and low and sing:

Black clouds gather
My heart flutters.

Ammajan would sing Amir Khusro's *malhar*:

جھولا کن ڈارو سے امریاں

Put up the swing in Ammrian, O friend.

When the rain increased and we were soaked from head to toe, we would dash for shelter under the awning by the verandah, while droplets of water dripped from our hair.

Sawani

The word *sawani* is derived from the month of *sawan*, the monsoon. This was a time for romance, for the quickening of life and new grass and leaves springing. In the olden days it was the custom that when the bride was brought home to her husband's house, her in-laws celebrated *sawani* according to their means. This frequently coincided with the rainy season, when there was a constant sprinkling and the centre of the festivities was the ritual of the *jhoola*. The bride and groom, dressed in their finery, were made to sit together on the swing while the young girls, friends and relatives, laughed, teased, and sang *malhar*. *Chunrees* and bangles were distributed among all the women guests.

An Account of Sawani Celebrations in the Words of Apa Jan[4]

'My *Sawani* was celebrated in 1921 with great pomp and show by Nawab Hamid Ali Khan. Arrangements were made to have total *purdah* in the Benazir Gardens with a *qanat*, all around, surrounded by guards. In those days, *mirasans*, musicians, dancers and singers came from different cities to perform in the celebrations at the Court of Rampur. The famous Gauhar Jan of Calcutta, Zohra Bai Agre-walli, and Rajeshwari Bai from Benaras are a few of the performers whose names come to mind.

'In short, guests began assembling in the Benazir Gardens early in the morning. All the women from the family and the *begumaat* from the Royal Fort, were present. Small tents had been pitched under the trees and swings were suspended from the branches of mango trees. Some distinguished visitors stayed at the royal guest-house. For His

Highness, there was a *chohel choba,* a special moveable pavilion, which was erected wherever he chose to stop, after a stroll. From every tree you could hear people singing a different *malhar.* Trays with a variety of snacks had been provided for the guests. There were arrays of delicious dishes elaborately laid out on the tablecloths too. In those days, even the *kaharis* were in glittering attire. They were laden in silver ornaments from head to foot, wore *patta-patti lehngas,* with brightly coloured *cholis,* and red or light green *chunree dupattas.* They distributed dry *mehndi* in brass trays and bowls. Thousands of multicoloured *chunrees* were given to all the guests too, including the staff. I also had *mehndi* applied to my hands and feet. I was in a *karchobi* suit with an *orhni* of tissue, shot with green stripes, which had been specially woven in Benaras. On my feet I wore golden sandals with gold bells that tinkled with every step.

'In a portico of the Benazir Palace, a swing with multicoloured cords had been set up, its *ganga-jamini,* gold and silver plank swaying to and fro. The *Waliahed,* Nawabzada Raza Ali Khan arrived dressed in a *kemkhab sherwani* and *karchobi* cap. All the ladies were present; some were in *purdah* and they watched the proceedings from behind bamboo screens. We were both seated in the swing for the recitation of *Bismillah.* Nawab Hamid Ali Khan performed a *nichawar* and threw one hundred and one *ashrafis* over me; others followed suit. Then His Highness gave the cord of the swing a gentle push. That was when the excitement really began: the singing women immediately broke into one of His Highness's compositions in their melodious voices. I still remember a line from that song:

آج دلہن کو جھولا جھلائیں
کالی کالی بدری گھر گھر گھر آئیں

Today we make the bride swing in the jhoola
As black clouds slowly gather

'An elaborate programme of songs and dance followed. Gauhar Jan danced the *kathak*. The gathering ended in the early hours of the morning with musicians performing the *raag bhairavi*.'

This was Apa Jan's account. I too have a vague recollection of that *Sawani*. There were lots of swings in the mango trees, crowds of guests, and the bride's swing was hung with bells; we sisters sat on it with the bride. His Highness's voice echoed in the air and left everyone awe-stricken.

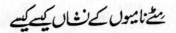

Signs of so many illustrious ones have gone with the wind

NOTES

1. Her Highness Rafat Zamani Begum of Rampur, *Jab Mein Dulhan Bani*, first written for All-India Radio, Rampur.
2. One of the nicknames by which Papa was known.
3. The nickname by which Raza Ali Khan was known, as a child.
4. Written in a letter to me in 1985.

✥ 4 ✥

THE BIRTH OF APA JAN'S FIRST CHILD AND RAMPUR'S FUTURE HEIR NAWABZADA MURTAZA ALI KHAN

Nawab Hamid Ali Khan celebrated the birth of his grandson, Murtaza Ali Khan, with grand festivities. On the beautiful, spring-like morning of 22 November 1923, the sound of cannons created a wave of excitement everywhere in the state of Rampur. This child was very special to Nawab Hamid Ali Khan and he prostrated himself before Allah in gratitude. He lovingly called the baby Bacchan, by which he came to be widely known.

Cheers of felicitations and good wishes filled the air. The flag was raised on Khasbagh Palace. The astrologer immediately began looking at the child's horoscope; the astronomer consulted his books; and the soothsayer studied the child's stars. Drums were beaten publicly, the *shehnai* broke into *raag durbari* and the dancers, singers, and musicians began their performances. The words of the song were:

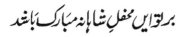

May this royal assembly bring you good fortune.

Members of the royal household and government officials presented their *nazr*, in homage. Crowds formed at the gates and a steady stream of guests continued all day. The royal treasury showered endowments on the people. Dance and music programmes were announced for both the *mardana* and the *zenana*. It was a time of fabulous celebrations.

My mother said that the *zenana* was lit up like a fairyland that day. The palace was packed with guests. The adornment of the *begumaat*—their *karchobi orhnis*, *farshi* pyjamas with *tukri* work, their *naths* and *teekas*, added to the magical setting. They all waited for Nawab Sahib so that they could offer their good wishes and present their *nazr*. Apa Jan, dressed like a bride, was seated on a *chaparkat*, a golden canopy bed. She wore a beautiful *nath,* studded with pearls, and a gem-studded band stretched across her forehead. Her child, wearing a *kurta* with *lachka* stitching and a pyjama, a jewelled band on his forehead looked as beautiful as the moon. The *mirasans* in their *peshwazes* decorated with spangled ribbons and *go'ta*, danced the *keharwa* and, along with other songs, sang the one composed by His Highness.

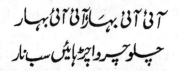

Spring is here, spring is here
Friends, let's go and present the charva

The ceremony of the *chouchak,* was arranged by the family and the nobles of the city. This was when the baby's layette was sent by his maternal relatives; it consisted of *kurtas, topi, achkan, razai, dullai,* toys, a swing, silver utensils, a cow adorned with silver jewellery and a baby lamb. Accompanied by a procession with marching bands, trumpets, family friends and singers, it made its way past our house.

Then that wonderful day arrived, when Apa Jan brought Bacchan Sahib to her parents' home, for the first time. How grand were the preparations that preceded her arrival! White floor-coverings were laid everywhere, *khatolis* were placed in every corner, and special arrangements were made for the male visitors to stay in the *mardana*. My sister and I wore heavily ornamented suits and waited at the doorway. A division of the army and a guard of honour was formed up outside. Canopies had been set up. Soon five or six limousines pulled into the driveway. Darogha Kallan Sahib went forward and helped Apa Jan get down from the car. Apa Jan was wearing a very heavy *karchobi* suit and had a *sehra* on her face. She carried the baby on a red velvet baby cloth. Bacchan Sahib was in a *kurta* decorated with *lachka* and *go'ta*. A band studded with diamonds covered his forehead. Ammajan and Dadimayya led Apa Jan to a silver *khatoli* and then coins were tossed over her and the baby. The *mirasans* were singing songs loudly and melodiously.

Papa arrived in the *zenana* and was overjoyed to see his daughter and his grandson. He presented Apa Jan with a beautiful set of jewellery, diamond buttons for his son-in-law, and a *kalghi*, a gem-studded aigrette, for Bacchan Sahib.

Bacchan spent his early years in the loving care of his paternal grandfather. He was seven when his grandfather departed from this world. Apa Jan felt the loss deeply and my father grieved at losing his appreciative sovereign and dear friend.

زمینِ چمن گل کھلاتی ہے کیا کیا

بدلتا ہے رنگ آسماں کیسے کیسے

The earth's garden produces such flowers,
Such varying shades the sky is recast in.

❖ ❖ ❖

THE ROYAL HOUSEHOLD
OF NAWAB HAMID ALI KHAN

I remember Nawab Hamid Ali Khan quite well. I was about ten at the time and Bahan Fakhra was eleven. His splendour and grace were that of a king. What grandeur and dignity he emanated! His voice was so commanding and forceful that it held everyone in awe even from a distance. He was of average height and he would usually be attired in a coat with a high collar and studded with jewelled buttons; on his head he usually wore a velvet Rampuri cap.

Once he visited the *zenana* with Papa. While he was engaged in a conversation with Ammajan and Dadimayya who were both behind a curtain, Papa said that the girls were ready to present their salutations. He bid us come forward. Both Bahan Fakhra and I approached him somewhat timidly. We offered our salutations and silently stood to one side. He glanced at us with affection, motioned us to sit down and then proceeded to ask, 'Girls, will you write "Abban" for me?' My father's relatives and close friends called my father Abban Mian. In my nervousness I misspelled the word. He exclaimed 'Good heavens! She doesn't know how to spell her father's name!'

Nawab Hamid Ali Khan was a remarkable man, accomplished, fluent in Urdu, Persian, Arabic and English; a man of letters with a personality that

19. Nawab Faizullah Khan of Rampur. He built the Qila-e-Mualla and began the personal collection of manuscripts now housed in the Raza Library.

20. Nawab Mohammed Saeed Khan of Rampur.

21. Nawab Yusuf Ali Khan of Rampur, Mirza Ghalib's pupil. He welcomed scholars, artists and poets to his court and built up a rare collection of manuscripts. These are all in the Raza Library today, together with the correspondence between Nawab Yusuf Ali Khan and Mirza Ghalib.

22. Jama Masjid, Rampur city, today.

23 Pyare Mian, the court eunuch, in uniform

24. Post-independence view of Hamid Manzil in the Qila-e-Mualla. This is where the investiture ceremonies and *durbars* used to take place before Partition. It now houses the Raza Library.

25. Post-independence view of Hamid Manzil, repainted.

26. Rang Mahal in the Qila-e-Mualla *circa* 1950s. Mehfils and musical gatherings used to take place here.

27. The portico or *deohri*, of Macchi Bhawan in the Qila-e-Mualla. This building housed the private apartments of the ruler. The La'al Purdah *deohri* was next to it.

28. Khasbagh Palace, *circa* 1950s, 'D' Block. Guests stayed here during the reign of Nawab Raza Ali Khan.

29. Khasbagh Palace, *circa* 1950s, 'C' Block. The original part of the palace, built by Nawab Hamid Ali Khan; it included a banqueting hall and ballroom.

30. Khasbagh Palace, *circa* 1950s, 'A' Block, was built by Nawab Raza Ali Khan and housed the private apartments of the Nawab and Begum of Rampur.

31. Khasbagh Palace, *circa* 1950s, across the front lawn, showing the meeting between the two distinct architectural styles of 'A' Block (right) and 'C' Block.

32. Sahibzada Sir Abdus Samad Khan, 1914.

33. Bismillah Ceremony of Nawabzada Murtaza Ali Khan aged four years and four months, at Khasbagh Palace Rampur, 1927.

Front row: From L to R. Nawabzada Abdul Karim Khan of Rampur, a Prince of Malerkotla, Not Identified, Nawab Sir Amiruddin Ahmed Khan of Loharu, Maharajah of Alwar, Nawab Hamid Ali Khan of Rampur, Maharajah of Bikaner, Maharajah of Dholpur, Nawab of Malerkotla, Nawab of Palanpur, Prince of Malerkota, Nawabzada Jaffer Ali Khan of Rampur.

Second row: Sahibzada Qamar Shah Khan, Sahibzada Abdul Majeed Khan, Sahibzada Abdul Wahid Khan, Sahibzada Rashiduzzafar Khan, Sahibzada Abdul Jalil Khan, Raja Ghazanfar Ali, Maulana Shaukat Ali, Nawab Ismail Khan, Sahibzada Mahmood Ali Khan, Sahibzada Sir Abdus Samad Khan.

34. The visit of the Viceroy, Lord Irwin, to Rampur *circa* 1929.

35. Nawab Hamid Ali Khan of Rampur.

attracted thinkers, philosophers, religious leaders of both the Ahl-e-Sunnat and the Fiqah Ja'afria and also well-known poets and writers. He conducted discussions with all of them, provided exemplary hospitality to all his guests, and despite his fiery temper, was generous to a fault.

❖ ❖ ❖

WELCOMING BEGUM ATTIYA FAIZI
RAMPUR 1924

During the reign of Nawab Hamid Ali Khan, the legendary Attiya Begum Faizi Rahamin and her sister, the Begum of Janjeera came to Rampur. They were regaled with honours and were invited to tea at our house. I remember that Papa ordered that we girls appear in *farshi* pyjamas and pay our respects, although Bahan Fakhra and I were both very young. She was overjoyed to see us and praised the embroidery and the artistry of the *mughalani* who had made the clothes. I remember that she said, 'This is the true royal dress of the Muslim era.' She cherished the cultural traditions of a bygone age.

God had blessed her with such graces. She was fluent in Persian, Arabic and English. Her husband, Faizi Rahamin was a renowned artist who had established an organization in Bombay to encourage the growth and development of art, poetry, music and painting. She mixed with ruling princes and literary figures. She was a wonderful conversationalist and knew thousands of couplets by heart, which she would quote with ease.

Nawab Hamid Ali Khan had met her in Bombay and had the honour of calling her 'sister.' She corresponded with Bernard Shaw. Maulana Shibli Naumani was so impressed with her that he has written

Persian *ghazals* addressed specifically to her. What greater honour could there be?

عطیہ میرا ہر رونگٹا اور ہر موئے بدن تمہاری توصیف اور تعریف کا ایک شعر ہے

Attiya, every pore and every hair on my body is a poetic verse to exalt you and to praise you.

– Shibli Naumani,
9 August 1909

✤ 5 ✤

QILA-E-MUALLA
THE ROYAL FORT, RAMPUR

از نقش و نگار درو دیوار شکسته
آثار پیداست صنادید عجم را

The ornamentation that remains on the crumbling walls
Speaks of the great men of Ajam.

The foundations of the Qila-e-Mualla, the Royal Fort, were laid in 1774, during the reign of Nawab Faizullah Khan. Subsequent rulers made changes and additions, according to their needs. The present day picture of the Qila differs from what it was in the past.

Nawab Mohammad Saeed Khan and Nawab Yusuf Ali Khan are buried next to the men's *imambara*. Nawab Mohammad Saeed Khan, the ruler of Rampur from 1840–59, was succeeded by Nawab Mohammad Yusuf Ali Khan. His son, Nawab Kalb-e-Ali Khan, in turn assumed the reigns of government in 1865; he was very fond of architecture. He gave special attention to developments in the city and the embellishments of the Qila itself. The gate of the fort, an imposing structure, came to be known as Dar-e-Daulat.

Mir Mohammad Zaki the well-known poet has written of the gate thus:[1]

خسرو نام آور دعرش احتشام   ساختہ دروازۂ رفعت نشاں
گفت چنیں سال بنا یش زکی   ہست در دولت و باب السلام

The great king has built a magnificent gate,
Zaki exclaims this is the door of fortune, the gate of protection.

In the time of Nawab Kalb-e-Ali Khan, an elaborate fair which became renowned all over Hindustan, was held in the Benazir Gardens. Amir Mina'i says:

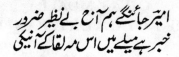

Amir, we will go to the Benazir today,
It is rumoured the beauteous one will be there.

Nawab Mushtaq Ali Khan, who had a very short reign from 1887 to 1889, first introduced English architectural styles in Rampur. On the advice of General Azimuddin Khan, he summoned Mr Wright, a noted European engineer, from Lucknow. An extremely able man, he was given the post of Chief Engineer, showered with special honours and gifts, and the gate of the Qila, known as Wright Gate, was named after him. His bungalow still survives in Rampur and several buildings of English design were built by him, during that period.

Nawab Hamid Ali Khan assumed the reigns of government in 1896. His reign was characterized by such splendour and majesty that it reminded people of the past glories of Oudh. Rampur's patronage of literature, the arts, and music, gained renown all over Hindustan, as did its sumptuous royal cuisine. He harboured a special interest in architecture and built several fine buildings. The Qila-e-Mualla, whose area is two miles square feet, was rebuilt. Its design is reminiscent of the La'al Qila, in Delhi. Towering battlements surround the Qila on all sides. The residence of the ruler, Macchi Bhawan, which has a pair of golden fish as an emblem on top of the tower, was extended, as was Rang Mahal where celebrations and musical gatherings took place. Hamid Manzil took the place of Khurshid Manzil and was a magnificent palace where the *durbars* were held. Mr Wright worked very hard during the construction of Hamid Manzil and other buildings within the Qila.

The walls of the Qila and its two gates have been cast with red brick, and both the Wright Gate and Hamid Gate are impressive structures, so tall that an elephant could pass through them with ease. Right above the gate is the *naubat khana*, the place where according to the custom, drums were struck both in the morning and at sunset. Wright Gate, commonly used for daily thoroughfare, faces the post office, while Hamid Gate, which was used only on special occasions, is in front of the law courts. Two armed lancers stood guard on horseback at the entrance.

The men and women's *imambaras* were also re-done. In the *zenana*, there were several *mahalseras*, some so spacious that they included small gardens within their confines. The main gardens in the Qila, exquisitely landscaped, were dotted with marble and bronze statues. There was enough space in the large compound for *imambaras*, mosques, store rooms, kitchens, libraries, offices and quarters for male workers. Living quarters here, housed the ADCs, the secretaries, the fort commandant, the medical attendants, chefs, clerical staff, musicians and dancers, *khwajasaras,* professional story-tellers, *marsia* and *soz* reciters, the court poet, Zamin Sahib, one hundred and twenty-two cooks and the same number of torch bearers. In addition, there were messengers, domestics, ushers, mace-bearers, and innumerable other workers and helpers that inhabited the Qila.

The *zenana* also bustled with women attendants. There were the personal maids and nurses, but there were a host of others too, including *Saiyidanis* who supervised the seamstresses and looked after the *imambara*; the *toraydarnis* who distributed customary portions of food and sweets on religious occasions and carried them on trays to the neighbours; the *mammayein* who were the guardians of the *zenana* entrance way; and the *chobdarnis* who were the heralds, always walking as a pair, in front of Apa Jan, on ceremonial occasions, to announce her presence. Each section of the household, such as the kitchens or the wardrobe, or the *imambara*, was supervised by a *darogha.*

Among them, the highest in rank was Darogha Kallan Sahib, a lady who was unique in many ways. She possessed a special understanding of the mercurial nature of court life and was so well attuned to the royal temperament, that she was able to provide solutions to the most difficult problems. Due to her tact, Nawab Hamid Ali Khan's temper never reached its height and punishment was rarely meted out. Her face bespoke a keen intelligence, her conversation was always interesting, her manner cultured and personable.

A virtuous and religious lady, she always had a *tasbih* in her hand. In her young days, she must have been attractive. She always wore a white dupatta draped over her head, a white shirt and a coloured *farshi pa'incha.* She was also in charge of the *deohri*, the entrance way to the *zenana* and had a room nearby. This area was known as the La'al Purdah, because a heavy, quilted red curtain hung behind the doors to the *zenana* entrance. All the women lived behind this, including Darogha Kallan Sahib.

She was required to keep a watch on the comings and goings of visitors and had a delicate job to perform, one involving a great deal of trust. She enjoyed the same status during the reign of Nawab Raza Ali Khan and she claimed the honour of standing next to Apa Jan in the *zenana durbar* and collecting, in a brocade pouch, the gold *ashrafis*, presented as homage.

Visiting the Fort

Our visits to the Qila, for special occasions in the olden days, were so claustrophobic, they seem like something from a storybook now. The Shahi Mahal, Macchi Bhawan and La'al Purdah constituted an exclusive area, where no one dared enter: only a handful of people were allowed to come to the La'al Purdah in their carriages or cars. The rules of *purdah* were so strict here, that even the people working there had to watch every step. There was a *Kumandaan* Sahib or Commandant who looked after the *deohri*. As soon as our car had passed through, he used to call out orders to erect the *qanat* higher than the *deohri* walls and close the gates; only then could we alight and enter the *zenana*, beyond the La'al Purdah.

The worst moment came when the music and celebrations came to an end, in the early hours of the morning: it was winter, we were shivering with cold, tired, sleepy, irritable and knew the hazards of just being in the awful *deohri*. We had to wait for hours in an ante-room before going home because a strict protocol had to be observed.

The procedure was that Darogha Kallan Sahib would summon the *mammayein*, ask them to call the *Khwajasara*, the Court Eunuch, and ask him to seek His Highness's permission for the guests to leave. The

Khwajasara would then convey this to the *Kumandaan* Sahib. He, in turn, would look for the Household Secretary. When he was found, he would convey the message to His Highness's ADC. The ADC's job was particularly tricky. He had to wait for an opportune moment to seek due permission.

Finally, through the same rigmarole, the *mammayein* would come back to Darogha Kallan Sahib and announce, 'Permission granted'. The guests would sigh with relief and move rapidly towards the car. The *Khwajasara* would carefully check identities.

The *mammayein* then called out to the *Kumandaan* Sahib, 'Open the gates!' He answered, 'Shall I open the gates?' This exchange was repeated three times, till the *qanat* was finally removed, the gates opened, and the car's engine whirred. What a relief it was to be released!

In the days of Nawab Hamid Ali Khan, these precautions were taken, in case any of His Highness's ladies tried to escape amongst the crowd at the gathering. This was mercifully discontinued after the first year or two of Nawab Raza Ali Khan's reign, because he was a more enlightened ruler and the restrictions were gradually relaxed.

❖ ❖ ❖

RAZA LIBRARY, RAMPUR

The mention of the library brings Hamid Manzil to mind. Hamid Manzil was constructed during Nawab Hamid Ali Khan's reign and was named after him. Situated in the confines of the Qila-e-Mualla, this building is an unusual example of Mughal architecture. At one time, it was the Nawab of Rampur's official residence. The Royal *Durbar* was held in the main hall whose ceilings and columns were decorated with ornate designs and motifs; its huge chandelier of hand-cut Bohemian glass, is particularly noteworthy. This is also the palace that now accommodates one of Hindustan's most renowned libraries.

The library began two hundred years ago, as the personal collection of the first Nawab of Rampur, Nawab Faizullah Khan. Subsequent rulers added to the holdings in this library, developing it into a treasure trove of extremely precious books.

During the turmoil in 1857, when Delhi and Lucknow both suffered great devastation, scholars and artists fled with little else except some priceless books and rare pictures in their possession. In those days Nawab Yusuf Ali Khan, who was Mirza Ghalib's student, was the ruler of Rampur. He held learned men in great honour. He gave refuge to all those who came to him for help from the war-torn cities of Delhi and Lucknow. By the time his son, Nawab Kalb-e-Ali Khan, became the ruler, a most impressive collection of rare books, manuscripts and pictures had been accumulated in the library. During the reign of Nawab Raza Ali Khan, which began in 1930, the library gained worldwide fame among oriental and Islamic scholars.

He appointed Maulana Imtiaz Ali Arshi as the library's custodian. This was a stroke of good fortune for the library. Arshi Sahib's devotion to books, his passion for knowledge and his special enthusiasm for research was known to all. He was a scholar of international repute and I often saw him in Rampur, deep in conversation with Apa Jan. After his death, his son, Akbar Ali Khan Arshizada, took his place

Not only is this library the largest in Hindustan in terms of space, it is also the largest by way of its holdings.[2] Books in Arabic rank at the top, followed by nearly six thousand texts in Persian, two thousand in Urdu and some in Pashtu and Turkish as well.

A rare manuscript of the Quran, penned by Ibn-e-Muqulla Baghdadi, which is over a thousand years old, is among its valued treasures. Another, even more rare manuscript of the Quran, written on leather and dating back to the first century Hijri, is said to have been penned by the revered hands of Hazrat Ali *Karamullah Waj'hu* in the Kufic script.

Mirza Muhammad Haris Badakhshi's *Tarikh-e Mohammedi* (*The History of Mohammed*), written during the reign of Aurangzeb, is another notable text to be found here. The library also contains the exchange of letters between Mirza Ghalib and his pupil, Nawab Yusuf Ali Khan of Rampur and includes the corrections that he made in the Nawab's verse. There are some other interesting texts in the library as well. The court storytellers compiled *dastaans* in the tradition of *Talism-e-Hoshruba* and *Dastaan-e-Amir Hamza* which, written in their own hand, can be found here. Innumerable scholars, poets and historians have made use of the Raza Library at Rampur, but some are of special note: Maulana Shibli Naumani, Hakim Ajmal Khan, Allama Najmul Ghani Khan Rampuri, Maulana Abdul Majid Daryabadi and Sayyed Suleiman Nadwi, are a few of the well-known and well-respected scholars who used the library extensively.

Recently, Apa Jan's, son Nawabzada Zulfiqar Ali Khan, popularly known as Mickey Mian, was the library's custodian. He lost his life in a tragic accident, leaving behind a terrible sense of loss among us all, but by God's Grace, his son is now carrying the torch. I believe that the library belonging to the rulers of Loharu, has also been added to the Raza Library.

NOTES

1. This couplet employs a hidden method of numerology which gives the date of construction, as approximately 1282 AH.
2. Raza Ali Abidi, *Kutub Khana*, Published by Sang-e-Meel Publications, Lahore, 1995.

✤ 6 ✤

EID FESTIVITIES IN RAMPUR

In Rampur, Eid-ul-Fitr and Eid-ul-Azha were both celebrated with much enthusiasm and fervour. The *naubat* used to be played at the gates of the Qila-e-Mualla and the musicians of Rampur presented the ceremonial *mubarakbadi* in *raag durbari*. The *zenana* and *mardana durbars* were held with great splendour. Musicians, dancers and singers provided entertainment in Macchi Bhawan, while in the *zenana* the *mirasans* danced the *keharwa* to the accompaniment of festive songs. The ladies, dressed in *farshi pyjamas* and bedecked in all their jewellery including a *nath* and a *teeka*, would appear in the *durbar*.

Eid-ul-Azha is celebrated on the 10th Zilhaj to commemorate Hazrat Ibrahim's sacrifice. Every Muslim is deeply affected by this Islamic ritual, the Hajj-e-Batullah. After special Eid-ul-Azha prayers, in each household, a sacrifice of a cow, lamb, or camel is offered and the meat distributed among friends and relatives, but the largest portion is for those who are not well to do.

Eid-ul-Fitr marks the end of Ramzan, the holy month of fasting and prayer and it is celebrated on the 1st of Shawwal, the new month. *Fitra* (charity) is collected and distributed. The months in which Eid-ul-Azha and Eid-ul-Fitr fall, are very blessed and usually wedding dates are decided at the time. After the engagement ceremony a special gift called *Eidi* is sent for the bride-to-be, comprising of *mehndi*, bangles, a silk suit or saree, dry fruit, *sewayyan*, crystallized sugar and floral adornments. On the day of Eid, children are the happiest because they get new clothes, new shoes, and also gifts of money from their elders.

After the Eid prayers, on Eid-ul-Fitr, my father always opened his fast with sweet *sheer khurma*, as did everyone else. He would then go to the *mardana*, to meet his relatives and friends. I clearly remember the Eid of my childhood. *Purdah* was an integral part of our lives, there was a lot of leisure time on our hands, and relatives, servants, and attendants filled the house. The *paharwallis* and the *mughlanis* used to tell such interesting tales. The cleverest and the wisest of the *mughlanis* was Yaquti Mughlani. Her stitching was superb. She was the one who did all the shopping for our Eid clothes. She would bring materials from the cloth merchant and the lacemaker, the *go'ta garh*, for our approval; that's how easy it was to for the women to do their shopping. The suit to be worn on Eid was always very colourful and stylish. The *churidar* pyjama was of satin or raw silk, the waistcoat of velvet or satin and with it we wore either a coloured wrinkled *dupatta* or a georgette *dupatta*. The *kurta* and *dupatta* were always edged with glittering *go'ta*.

The *sewayyan* were usually made at home. There used to be a strange kind of wooden contraption. Kneaded farina or dough would be placed in a special compartment and then the lid would be pressed down hard on it. The *sewayyan* would appear in bunches below. The strands were separated by hand and spread out on the branches of trees. This required skilful manoeuvring so that the strands wouldn't break or become tangled.

Sewayyan cooked in syrup are called *kiwami sewayyan* and need to have four times the usual amount of sugar. Those with less sugar, called *muzaffir,* are the variety cooked with saffron. There are also several ways to prepare *sheer khurma* in milk. All these were displayed on the *dastarkhan* on Eid, decorated with flecks of fine silver leaf, and served in silver dishes.

On Chand Raat, the evening before Eid, I remember that we would stand on the rooftop for hours waiting to see the new moon. The moment the moon was officially sighted in Rampur, the cannons were fired, followed by great joy and excitement: preparations for applying *mehndi* to our hands, the wait for the bangles, the sheen and glitter of garments to be worn the next day, the fragrance of *sewayyan* travelling to every corner of the house. White *chandni* would be spread in the *dalaan* and laid with white *masnads* and bolsters, with a *dastarkhan* in the centre; silver *paandaans,* *khaasdaans,* and *itrdaans* were ceremoniously arranged—and, how they glittered!

On both Eids, Ammajan would distribute *Eidi* to all the *paharwallis.* Around this time the bangle-seller, would appear with her basket of bangles lined with red twill. We would all crowd round her. After we had selected our bangles and put them on, we stood up and offered our *salaams* to the bangle seller. I think this is an omen of good luck, because bangles are the symbol of *suhag,* of happiness in your future married life.

A steady stream of guests kept everyone busy in the house. We always succeeded in collecting a lot of cash, as *Eidi*. In those days the giving of *Eidi* was a ritual and had nothing to do with money or riches.

❖ ❖ ❖

OUR HOME, ROSAVILLE

Papa was the Chief Minister of Rampur State. The two-storey house we lived in had been constructed according to his specifications. The architecture of the house reflected a combination of both western and eastern styles. There was a courtyard, verandahs and bedrooms in the *zenana* with rooms on the upper floor also. Within the boundary wall was a huge garden. On both sides of a stone pathway, there were flowering bushes of scented white flowers: *mogra, chambeli, motia, bela,* and *madan-ban.* The swing was always ready for use. There were servants everywhere. Dadimayya and her entourage, along with some other relatives, also lived with us, as did my cousins, Hajjo Apa and Kamman Apa, who were my age. Other cousins, such as Anjum Zamani Begum and Nayyar Zamani Begum, visited us regularly. They were all my playmates. We used to celebrate the weddings of our dolls and had so much fun. What a wonderful time that was! The days were like Eid, the nights were like Shab-e-Baraat!

My three brothers, Yusuf, Yunus, and Yaqub spent their childhood years with us. We all played together. But when the boys grew up, they were shifted to the *mardana.* Master Alam Buksh from the Aligarh University was appointed their tutor. He also taught them English, while Munshi Shaida Ali Khan came to instruct them in Persian. Swimming, target-practice, horse riding—they were taught all these skills. At a young age, the three brothers were together at the English House School, Aligarh. Later they were admitted to different schools.

The land surrounding the house was extensive: it included mango groves, a mosque, stables, a washerman's *ghat,* and servant quarters. Two *munshis* from our lands and villages kept the accounts,

Darogha Syed Hasan Shah being entrusted with giving out of salaries to the employees and with the management of grain. The English kitchen was run under the supervision of Faiz Rasool. At breakfast, Papa was often with visitors and friends, including Maulvi Sa'adullah, his childhood friend and companion. Nathu Singh was Papa's personal valet and understood all his likes and dislikes.

Papa had a special rose garden constructed in front of his bedroom where roses blossomed and danced in the breeze. He loved roses and for that reason the house came to be known as Rosaville.

The education my sister and I received was according to both western and eastern systems. An English governess introduced us to an English education, while Maulvi Ashfaq Hussain taught us Urdu and Persian. We did not observe *purdah* in front of Maulvi Sahib, but a chaperone always stayed with us in the room when he was teaching. We grew up in *purdah* according to the cultural mores prevalent at the time. The rituals of *milad* and *nazr* and *niaz,* were frequently conducted in the *zenana* because Ammajan faithfully prayed and observed Ramzan and other religious conventions.

Celebrations in connection with Nawab Raza Ali Khan's investiture began in the October of 1930. Around this time, my sister, Bahan Fakhra fell ill. The doctors suggested a change of climate. Ammajan decided to take us to Dehra Dun where Papa had bought a house. His sister, Shaukat Ara Begum—Phupi Amma—and her husband, Dr Saiduzzafar Khan—Phupa Abba—were already living in Dehra Dun.

A long time ago, Ammajan and her younger sister, Fakhar, Begum of Loharu, had agreed that if Ammajan had a daughter she would become engaged to her sister's son, Shehryar. By chance, Ammajan gave birth to Bahan Fakhra and both sisters agreed to this match.

My aunt Fakhar Begum chose the name Fakhra for my sister, because it was akin to her own name. Unfortunately, our young and beautiful aunt soon departed from this world, leaving behind small children.

In 1926, her husband, Nawab Aiz'uddin Ahmad Khan, the ruler of Loharu, popularly known as Azam Mirza, visited Rampur. He placed the Quran above Bahan Fakhra's head and said, 'She will be Shehryar's bride and my daughter-in-law.' Not too long afterward my uncle also departed from this world. Shehryar Mirza, assumed the title Nawab Aminuddin Ahmad Khan, but because he was a minor, his grandfather, Nawab Sir Amiruddin Ahmad Khan, popularly known as Farrukh Mirza, was appointed regent, having abdicated as ruler of Loharu long ago.

Bahan Fakhra was twelve when the engagement was formally announced. During this time, preparations for her trousseau commenced at our house. A festive air, common at the time of a wedding, prevailed. The jeweller arrived with ornaments encrusted with precious stones, the goldsmith was busy casting pure gold jewellery; the silversmith received orders to create silver vessels; the cloth merchant began sending bales of material—*atlus*, *qanavaiz*, and *girant*—to the *zenana*. The *go'ta garh* brought over all the trimmings from his shop: different varieties of gold and silver *lachka*, *banat*, *tui*, *kalli*, *kiran*, *muquesh*, *chutki*, *mur-murra*, *gokhru*, *salma-sitare*, and *anchal*. Such was their glitter that it dazzled the eyes!

The *go'ta garh* created tiny *zardozi ganga-jamni* florets on the curtains for the bridal bed and designed an embroidered *turanj*, a paisley, for each of the four corners of the awning. The man working on the *kamdani*, embroidered such delicate single florets with coiled skeins of gold or silver on the *dupatta*, that the heavy *kamdani* looked like stars glittering in the sky.

36. Rosaville *circa* 1950s.

37. From L to R: Yusuf, Yaqub and Yunus, *circa* 1922.

38. Mussoorie: (clockwise) Lady Abdus Samad Khan, Yusuf, Jahanara, Yaqub, Fakhra, Masud, Yunus, *circa* 1936.

Expert at cutting, the *mughalanis* began their work; nothing was measured, yet there was never a false move or a wasted cut. What new patterns they invented! The borders of the quilts, *dullai*s and the *farshi pyjamas* were particularly remarkable. It is also an art to create florets with silver and gold skeins: first a starched basting cloth is placed under the *lachka* and then, after the florets are cut out with scissors, they are stitched with *muquesh*. The placement of a colourful *jigri* in the centre of the florets gives the appearance of a garden bursting with flowers.

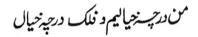

What plans I make,
And what the heavens have in store for me.

Call it coincidence or fate, or *kismet*, this match was not meant to be. On the one hand the trousseau was being prepared, on the other, Bahan Fakhra's illness was diagnosed as a mild tuberculosis. Doctors advised she should be taken to Switzerland for a checkup. In those days, it was unheard of, for a young *purdah-nashin* girl, to leave India. All of this created a misunderstanding which led to the termination of her engagement, to the great sorrow of Ammajan who was, and continued to be, very fond of Shehryar Mirza.

Meanwhile, another drama was beginning to unfold. Preparations began for my wedding with no regard for my young age. Nawab Raza Ali Khan expressed the desire that a *nikah* should take place between me and his nephew. As a matter of fact, the fabric for the ceremonial suit had already been cut! When Ammajan heard this, she was very distressed, but acting with great prudence and good sense, Ammajan took us to Dehra Dun, and thus the matter was finally closed.

DEPARTURE FROM RAMPUR
1931

We lifted our eyes at the world in amazement when we came out of *purdah*. The year was 1931. As our inhibitions slowly ebbed, we began to appreciate the life of freedom. Dehra Dun, which is a lush, green valley, one thousand and five hundred feet above sea level, is graced with beautiful gardens and an unlimited variety of trees. The fragrance of the cedars and the freshness in the air renewed our spirits. There is no shortage of flowers and fruits and there were charming picnic spots everywhere.

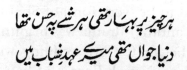

Spring was everywhere, everything was beautiful,
The world was young in the days of my youth.

We were all very happy to see our house, Rose Cottage. Some time ago, Papa had bought it, along with all the furnishings, from an Englishman. It had a large courtyard, rose bushes and, fresh green grass danced in the spacious garden; fruit trees of many different varieties dotted the landscape. Dehra Dun is especially well known for its lychees.

The house had badminton and tennis courts. Our governess, Mrs Mellzer, and our entire retinue of domestics had accompanied us from Rampur. My brothers, Yusuf, Yunus, and Yaqub came home frequently from Aligarh, their visits creating a lively atmosphere in the house. We are closely related to Brigadier Hamid Hussain. As a cadet at the Royal Military Academy in Dehra Dun, he was often a guest at Rose Cottage. He was sometimes accompanied by his fellow cadet, who later became General Habibullah Quli Khan Khattak of the Pakistan Army and who often recounted memories of those days, in later years.

My aunt and uncle, Phupi Amma and Phupa Abba, had been living in Dehra Dun for a long time. Their mansion was called Nasreen. Because of their presence in Dehra Dun, our stay there proved to be very relaxing and enjoyable. Nasreen was decorated with rare furnishings and the gardens, in particular, were extraordinary. They were crafted with such originality and beauty that people came from far and wide to see them. My sister and I were in love with the gardens. One could see such unusual things there: waterfalls, fountains spurting from ponds which housed colourful fish, parrots and other exotic birds flying around in screened cages, a pagoda from where one could view the garden in its entirety, bee houses, plants, and flowers of every imaginable variety.

An accomplished, learned man, Phupa Abba had very good taste, was extremely hospitable and sociable, and his house would always be filled with guests. Phupi Amma was a warm and cultured lady, a hostess whose planning skills were such that a single gesture from her was enough to make the staff operate flawlessly. We went to Nasreen every evening and played badminton. Phupa Abba made us run and laugh until we were breathless. Play would be followed by tea on the circular terrace. With what formality and elegance servants in livery and white gloves, used to present tea and delicious refreshments in a silver tea service and silver dishes!

Phupa Abba had had a very distinguished medical career. He had done his MRCP in Edinburgh and was among the founders of the King George's Medical College in Lucknow. He and Phupi Amma had been blessed with a son and a daughter. Their son, Sahibzada Mahmuduzzafar was in public school in England at the time, while the younger daughter, Hamida, was in the care of a governess.

In September 1931, Ammajan's youngest aunt, Nani Sahiba came to Dehra Dun because her daughter, Hajira Begum (Begum Mushtaq Ahmed Gurmani), was expecting. She gave birth to a daughter, Khalida Sultan, and celebrated the occasion with great ceremony. Our three brothers, Yusuf, Yunus, and Yaqub happened to be there at that time. Bahan Fakhra and I attended the festivities with Ammajan. I remember that our aunt, Hajira Begum, wore a jewel-studded *nath* and Khalida had a jewelled band across her forehead.

❖ ❖ ❖

TRAVEL TO EUROPE AND ENGLAND
1932

Bahan Fakhra was still ailing and the treatment in Dehra Dun had not produced satisfactory results. Finally the doctors suggested that Switzerland was the best place for the kind of treatment she required. Naturally Ammajan and my sister and I became very agitated at the thought of making such a long journey.

I was sixteen and Bahan Fakhra was a year older. How could Ammajan and two cloistered girls like us embark on a trip to Europe without being attended by a close male relative? We agonized over this. Fortunately, Phupa Abba was well-acquainted with England and Europe. The trip to Switzerland was arranged through him and finally this journey was undertaken in the care of Chacha Jan—Papa's brother—Sahibzada Abdul Wahid Khan, who took a six-month leave of absence from his work.

For some time we stayed in Ajmer. Chacha Jan's wife, Chachi Jan was travelling with her companion, Mrs Khan, whose daughter, Amy, was our age. She joined our party at that stage and thus there were seven of us on this journey, a veritable caravan. We left for Bombay by train. There were several family members present at the station to see us off, my Nani among them. She could not endure the pain of seeing us leave for such a distant country and also without *purdah*. She passed away a few days later.

The next morning we woke up to find ourselves at the Bombay train station. The platform was huge. Coolies thronged the area, vendors screamed their wares loudly, and crowds of passengers milled about. We were very nervous. Luckily, Thomas Cooke's staff took charge very rapidly and proceeded to make all the necessary arrangements. The company's name was inscribed on their caps and their uniforms, and they took care of us throughout our journey. The route to the Taj Mahal Hotel in Bombay was heavily populated; we saw more people here than we had ever seen before. The Taj Mahal Hotel is an exquisite structure, and the scenery along the sea was beautiful and extremely pleasing.

Our ship, the Caledonia of the Italian line, Lloyd Triestino, was anchored at the port. It looked beautiful from a distance. Colourful streamers flew in the breeze and, at night, the ship shimmered like a glowworm.

In a few days we were ready to depart. It was early morning. We stepped nervously on the narrow gangway along with a throng of other passengers and arrived on board the ship. Thomas Cooke's staff kept as close to us as shadows. First our luggage was deposited in the hold, then we went to see our berths. Ammajan, my sister and I, had one comfortable first class cabin, Chachi Jan and Chacha Jan, and Mrs Khan and Amy had their own separate cabins.

Shortly thereafter, the roar of the engines informed the passengers the ship was ready to depart; that was when we all went on deck. The ship slowly pulled out of the harbour; it was then that we finally realized that we were leaving our country.

We were well on our way, when the gong was struck for lunch. All of us assembled in the dining room, which was arranged with small tables. Handsome, well-groomed, uniformed waiters in white gloves, stood in a row alongside beautiful flower arrangements in silver vases. Italian food is delicious and we enjoyed our meal. At four o'clock we went on deck for tea. For dinner, it was customary for men to be dressed in dinner jackets and for the women to be attired in their best, from head to foot. The dining room was filled with lovely music played in the background by a band. After-dinner coffee was served in an elegant drawing room.

On board the ship, there were wonderful shops where everything one needed could be purchased at duty-free prices. After a long time, our ship docked at Port Said. We were overjoyed to see land after what had seemed like an age. Shopkeepers in Turkish caps came on board to sell their wares. We were more intrigued by their crafts and the merchandize they were exhibiting than in buying anything. We also went to see Port Said. Since the ladder was very steep and then with the the bobbing of the boat to contend with, getting off the ship and into the boats was a tricky business. The only thing I remember about Port Said was the *halwa* called Rahatul Hallsoom, an Egyptian sweet that I didn't like much.

Our journey ended at Genoa in Italy. We travelled by train from there to Venice. The world's most beautiful city left us in awe. Because it is built on canals, one can travel by water from one place to another, and the most commonly used mode of travel is the gondola, a slender and delicately-built boat. We were fascinated by the beautiful Italian leather which is world-renowned and were also amazed to see fine examples of Venetian glass, distinguished by its delicate craftsmanship and exquisite design. Milan, another Italian city, is famous for its extraordinary sculptures and the manufacture of glass products. The art galleries contain some of the best paintings by some of the world's most celebrated artists. We also visited an ancient monastery whose inhabitants have no connection with the outside world.

When we arrived in Lucerne we realized we were in Switzerland. I liked Geneva very much. A flourishing city, it is on a lake that greatly enhances its charm. At night, the reflection of the lights on the water, create a remarkably beautiful effect. On the way we also stopped briefly at Zurich and then stayed at Montana for a short while. One of the tourist attractions there was a snow-capped mountain peak, 15,000 feet above sea level, called Jung Frau. Thomas Cooke's staff made all the arrangements for us to go up the mountain. We sat in a strange kind of train, a funicular, to go all the way up. During the journey, we were frightened to find ourselves in the midst of mountains and a sheer drop below. At one stop we disembarked and found ourselves in a large room with glass windows. From there we could see the rays of the sun, shining upon massive, snow-clad mountain peaks. Since it was very cold, we did not stay there long.

Thick evergreen forests surrounded the small town near Montana where the sanatorium was situated. The pervasive fragrance of pinewood filled the air and revived and invigorated us. By God's Grace, Bahan Fakhra regained her health in one month and she was given gold injections as a cure.

Before leaving for England, Chacha Jan also took us to see Paris. We were there for two or three days. We sailed in a ferry in order to cross the English Channel. The weather was so bad and the water so choppy that our short passage seemed a lengthy ordeal. We were greatly relieved to see the cliffs of Dover. From here we journeyed by train to Ealing, where arrangements had been made for us to stay at a boarding house.

The boarding house was a pleasing, two-storey building with a small garden in an attached compound. I remember my bedroom; it was large, airy and well-furnished and all three of us slept there. A maid was in charge of keeping the room clean so we didn't have to do any work. The dining room and the drawing room were downstairs. English food is plain, but the puddings and tarts are delicious. There was a park nearby where we all spent quite a bit of time every day. The flowers, shady trees and different types of plants were a great joy to us. Ealing had some attractive shops, but because Chacha Jan didn't approve we didn't visit them too often. I was more fond of shopping than Bahan Fakhra.

Chacha Jan's sons, Hamid Bhai and Hadi Bhai who were both studying in England, spent their holidays with us. We enjoyed their company and visited all of London's historical sites with them. We saw Parliament House, the Tower of London, Crystal Palace, and also visited Madame Tussaud's wax museum, Kew Gardens and Hyde Park.

In July, on his way to Ottawa, Papa stopped over in London, to see us. He was to attend the Imperial Economics Conference as one of the four delegates who had been selected to represent India. They included Sir Abdullah Haroon. I remember meeting his wife, Lady Haroon, and his daughter, Daulat Hidayatullah, at the Dorchestor Hotel, where Papa was staying and where he invited us for tea. Papa also took us to dine at a fashionable London restaurant, Kit Kat. We were dazzled by the fashionable clothes, the jewellery, the cabaret show and the stage surrounded by elegant dining tables laid with cut glass and silver. The guests were dressed in white tie and tails.

Finally it was time for us to return home. Preparations for the long journey to India began. We left England on another Italian liner and when we glimpsed Bombay, after a journey of three weeks, our happiness knew no bounds. Kallu Khan, a senior *munsarrim*, the family steward, was at the port to receive us. We returned to Rampur with him.

We were surprised to see that several changes had taken place in our absence because Nawab Raza Ali Khan was a prince with liberal ideas. There were Englishmen everywhere. New factories had been set up. The state was on its way to progress. Unemployment had gone down, people were better off. The English liked the climate and the greenery of Rampur very much; beautiful fruit trees and shrubbery graced their homes.

In the evening, they played tennis or went riding. The dense forests provided ample opportunity for *shikar*. At night, there were lively dinner parties and the tinkling crystal glasses could be heard everywhere. My sister and I were no longer required to observe *purdah*, so we attended nearly every party in Papa's company. What fun life was then, how peaceful!

Alas! all that is no more. Only memories remain that we keep clasped to our hearts.

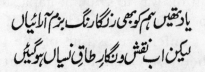

We too have known colourful reveleries of old,
But they have faded away to adorn the niche of memory.

❖ ❖ ❖

SNOW VIEW HOUSE, MUSSOORIE
1933–1934

In the first part of summer, Bahan Fakhra and I, travelled to Mussoorie with our brothers and Ammajan. Snow View House, where we stayed, was located on the same road as Charleville Hotel. I liked the verandah of this house very much; it was bright, with spacious, glazed windows which overlooked the huge garden, dotted with apricot trees. My Khala's daughter, Nawabzadi Sarwari Begum of Loharu, whom we called Choti Apa, was our guest. Her interesting conversation and the stories she had to tell, kept us riveted. She also sang very well, captivating everyone with renditions of *malhar* and *ghazals* in her melodious voice. One of the *ghazals* she sang was by her father, Nawab Azam Mirza.

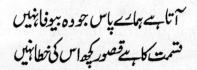

He would have come to me, he is not unfaithful,
It is a twist of fate, it is not his fault.

Sir Ross Masood, who was the grandson of Sir Syed Ahmad Khan, was related to Ammajan through his mother and was staying at Charleville Hotel. He was a very learned and a most distinguished personality. He would engage us in hours of fascinating conversation when he visited Ammajan, which was often. He was particularly fond of good food. He often requested special dishes, which Ammajan sent out to him regularly. He took us to a particularly memorable picnic, where the waterfall, Kempty Fall, was worth seeing.

Begum Shahid Hussain Kidwai visited Mussoorie during our stay there. Since Phupa Abba had known her family for a long time, we too were invited to visit. Her son, Rishad had just returned from Cambridge University and an elaborate celebration was held in his honour. Nearly all of the Mussoorie *beau monde* was present. What a grand affair that was.

In September the Mussoorie season comes to an end and everyone makes preparations to return home. We too were getting ready to go back to Rampur. Around this time I discovered that my hand had been promised to Rishad in marriage.

As soon as I returned to Dehra Dun from Mussoorie, I developed a high fever and the tickets for the onward journey to Rampur had to be cancelled. Everyone was extremely concerned about my condition. Blood tests revealed that my fever was due to a deadly attack of typhoid. In those days there was no treatment for typhoid; it is a miracle that I survived. The doctors had quite given up. The fever lasted three months and there was no letting up. During this time Phupa Abba and Dr Hoon took care of me tirelessly. Ammajan was constantly offering prayers for my health. God heard her prayers and I recovered from my illness, but since I was very weak and couldn't travel for another three months, Bahan Fakhra left for Rampur with Chacha Jan.

As it happened, Sahibzada Masuduzzafar, a young cousin of ours, was also staying at Rosaville. I returned to Rampur with Ammajan and after a short while we came to know that Bahan Fakhra was engaged to him. We were all overjoyed at this news. Nawab Raza Ali Khan of Rampur, took particular delight in this match because he and Masud Bhai were the same age and were good friends, with similar tastes. On 4 March 1935, amid colourful festivities, Bahan Fakhra's wedding to Masud Bhai took place.

✛ 8 ✛

BAHAN FAKHRA'S WEDDING
RAMPUR, 4 MARCH 1935

Spring was in the air and filled with the fragrance of *chambeli* and *motia*. The flowers were beginning to bloom, the burgeoning trees were resplendent with fresh, tiny buds. The breezes carried the happy message that a propitious moment was approaching.

This was the first wedding in our family in a very long time. The beating of the *naubat* began, the *dholak* was decorated, wedding songs and the verses of the *sehra*, echoed in the air. There were guests everywhere. This match was a source of joy for all the family, especially Nawab Raza Ali Khan, who handled the arrangements on the groom's side. The *baraat* arrived at our home with great pomp and ceremony.

All the young girls gathered for the ceremony of *dhol chapai*. Dressed in colourful, glittering attire, their anklets tinkling, they came and sat around the *dhol*, the drum. The family bangle-seller arrived with a basket full of bangles, covered with red cloth. All the girls slipped on the bangles; then they dipped their fingers in sandal paste and gave the *dhol* a tap, as a good omen, after which they received gifts of money. This was followed by a singing of the *suhag* along with

other wedding songs, the wedding ceremonies taking
on a spirited, festive tone in no time. I can only recall
a verse here and there from some of the very old
songs sung in those days:

راج دلاری گھونگھٹ کھول   میری ہریالی گھونگھٹ کھول

اک لکھ دوں گا دو لکھ دوں گا   میری ہریالی گھونگھٹ کھول

بنا بابا امول نوشہ بابا امول

گھونگھٹ کھول

My young one, lift up your veil
My dearest one, lift up your veil.
I'll give one lakh, I'll give two lakhs
My young one lift up your veil.

میری مائن بہت اچھا سا بنا لا سہرا

دولہا کم سن ہے کھلونا سا بنا لا سہرا

سہرے کا وقت ہوا دولہا کی ماں نے کہا

آج باندھے گا میرا راج دلارا سہرا

O flower-seller make me a beautiful sehra
The groom is young, make a sehra like a toy
It's time to put on the sehra, the groom's mother said
Today my dearly-beloved son will wear a sehra.

کاہے کو بیاہی بدیس رے سن بابل مورے

ہم تورے بابل بیلے کی کلیاں گھر گھر مانگی جائیں گے

سن بابل مورے

Why did you wed us so far away, listen O father mine
We, father are like chambeli buds O father
Wanted in every house, O father
Listen, O father mine.

A few days before the actual wedding day, Bahan Fakhra was secluded for the ceremony of *ma'yun.* Special sweets, big, round *peendiyan,* were made for the occasion. A corner of the room set aside for the bride, was decorated with a yellow coverlet and cushions, and a yellow curtain was hung across the area. The silver edging on the yellow fabric was breathtaking. Bahan Fakhra's suit was also yellow. Her innocent face was radiant. Married women performed the *manjha* ceremony. Sugary sweet balls and *ubtan* were placed on the bride's palms, a beautiful, shiny bracelet was tied around her wrist; fruits were deposited in her lap, and money to be later given away in charity, to the singing women, was thrown over her. They offered felicitations and sang:

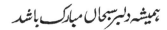

May the beloved live forever.

After the *arsi mus'haf,* Masud Bhai was summoned into the *zenana.* What a fine figure he presented! He looked resplendent in an outfit fashioned after the court dress, worn during the reign of Wajid Ali Shah, King of Oudh. His clothes glittered from head to foot. His coat, a *jama,* was made of gold *tamami* and it was edged by a *banat,* of five bands in different colours; it was worn over wide *kemkhab* trousers. On his feet were old-fashioned golden shoes; in his hand he held a *chaita,* a big purse made of the same *tamami* as the *jama.* On his head he wore a flat *puggaree,* wound with broad gold *go'ta* and his face was covered with a long, glittering *sehra,* a veil of gold and silver strands.

Bahan Fakhra made a beautiful bride. Her features were that of a Chughtai painting. She dazzled onlookers with her delicate figure, her lustrous and golden complexion, her gazelle-like eyes, enhanced by a *teeka*, glittering jewellery, a magenta head-covering and *karchobi* attire. Viewed through her long, diaphanous veil she looked like a fairy from *Koh Qaf*.[1]

At the time of the bride's departure, our three brothers, Yusuf, Yunus, and Yaqub were summoned into the *zenana*. Each one knotted tiny pieces of betel nut, strands of green grass, one rupee and turmeric chunks into all the four corners of the bride's *dupatta*, saying as they did so, 'Sister, I tie your virtue with this knot.'

Later, Papa had arranged a reception in the men's section. The gardens were blooming with fragrant flowers.

چمن سے بھرا باغ گل سے چمن   کہیں نرگس و گل کہیں یاسمن

چنبیلی کہیں اور کہیں موتیا   کہیں رائے بیل اور کہیں موگرا

کہیں ارغواں اور کہیں لالہ زار   جدی اپنے موسم میں سب کی بہار

کہیں زرد نسریں کہیں نسترن   عجب رنگ کے زعفرانی چمن

The garden full of flowers, flowers bursting with fullness,
Nargis in a corner, roses, jasmine too,
In a corner chambeli and motia as well,
Mustard vines in a corner and mogra too.
A dash of purple, tulip-cheeked tinge,
Each flower different in its beauty.
Yellow eglantine in a corner, white rose too,
What strange shades adorn the saffron-coloured gardens.

There were chairs and sofas laid on the carpets, small tables with silverware, sweets and cakes; liveried servants stood in attendance. There was a round terrace on one side of the garden where a band played. Soon the guests began to arrive. The

39. Fakhra as a bride. Her head is covered with an *orhni*, edged with different braids—a broad *go'ta, banat*, a narrow *go'ta* and *kiran* and she is in a robe, a *jama* of *tash*, spun gold and silk thread. She is wearing a *teeka* on her forehead and both a *nath* and a *keel*, in her nose.

40. Fakhra as a bride. She is wearing an *orhni*, over a *jama* of *tash* and a brocade *gharara*.

43. Sahibzada and Begum Masuduzzafar Khan at their wedding reception. She is wearing an *orhni* over a short jacket, a *shaluka*. The lower part of her *farshi pyjamas* has a design known as *parakah ki go't*. Her *karchobi* slippers, *ghaitli ki juti*, date back to the nineteenth century court of Oudh. He is in a brocade *sherwani*, a Rampur cap and a *churidar* or *arra pyjama*.

41. Masud at his wedding. He is dressed as a
    bridegroom, in an attire worn at the time of the
    Kings of Oudh in the nineteenth century. He is
    wearing a *jama* of *tash*, edged with *go'ta* and *banat*
    braids—as is his pyjama of Benarsi *zari* and *go'ta*.
    There is a Kashmiri *doshalla* on his shoulders and
    he is holding a large pouch, *chaita*, also made of
    tash, in one hand and, with the other he
    supporting a *sehra* strung with *motia* flowers,
    attached to his cap.

42. Masud wearing a *sehra*, strung with flower-shaped
    designs made of *go'ta* and attached to a *go'ta*
    covered cap, *mandeel*. He is holding a red chiffon
    handkerchief, with a gold braid.

44. Dinner party at Amar Singh Club, Srinagar. Second row, L to R: Jahanara, Ayesha of Cooch Behar (later Maharani Gayatri Devi of Jaipur), the Maharani of Cooch Behar, Nawab Khusro Jang, German guest, Ila of Cooch Behar (later Maharani of Tripura). First row, Yusuf, third from right. Third Row: Sahibzada Sir Abdus Samad Khan.

45. Sahibzadi Jahanara Begum, 1937.

46. Ayesha of Cooch Behar (later Maharani Gayatri Devi of Jaipur).

47. Maharajah Jagadipendra Narayan 'Bhaiya' of Cooch Behar.

48. Lady Abdus Samad Khan, the Maharani of Kashmir, and the Rani of Jasdan.

49. Jahanara with her father, Sahibzada Sir Abdus Samad
Khan on Eid Day in Kashmir. He is in *Durbar* dress.

50. The family home in Srinagar.

51. Isha'at Habibullah, 1942.

52. Isha'at and Jahanara Habibullah at their wedding, Lucknow.

53. The ladies who accompanied the *baraat* to Rampur for the wedding of Isha'at and Jahanara Habibullah. They are wearing *farshi pyjamas* and traditional jewellery. From L to R: Soraya Abbasi, Hamida Habibullah, Begum Inam Habibullah, Attia Habibullah (Attia Hosain), not identified, Qaisera Anwar Ali.

54. The wedding reception in Lucknow. Isha'at and Jahanara Habibullah, Begum Inam Habibullah with the Governor of the UP, Sir Maurice Hallet.

55. Sheikh Mohammed Habibullah, Taluqdar of Saidanpur (later, Vice-Chancellor of Lucknow University) dressed for an audience with Edward VII. London, 1905.

56. Begum Inam Habibullah.

Englishmen were dressed in morning coats and top hats and were accompanied by ladies in wide-brimmed hats and long white gloves; all the other men were in brocade *sherwanis.* Suddenly the guard presented arms and everyone stood up, to see His Highness, in a jewelled cap, walk in, smiling. Immediately after his arrival the bride and groom appeared and everyone moved forward to receive them. The bandmaster was English. The minute the newlyweds stepped into the garden the band struck up 'Here Comes the Bride.' Bahan Fakhra was now in a gold *karchobi* sari; a diamond stud, a *keel,* glittered in her nose. Masud Bhai looked elegant and handsome in his *sherwani* and cap. The cake-cutting ceremony took place, the laughter of the guests created a lively mood, and at the end of the ceremonies the bride and groom were sent off with good wishes, blessings and prayers.

In May, Papa left for England while we set out for Mussoorie again. This time we stayed at Crystal Bank, a house that was located on Camelback Road. Within days of our arrival, we heard that Nawab Raza Ali Khan would be visiting Mussoorie soon. His estate, Rampur House, was placed in readiness and the shopkeepers were ready with their wares. The halls at Hackman and Stifels restaurants were booked for parties, attended by all Mussoorie society. The best cabaret artists came from Europe. Shimmering saris, crowds of people dancing, the glitter of jewels and beautiful clothes, fine wines, and the laughter of the guests— the scene was like a page from a story book. After dinner at the Royal Suite in the Savoy Hotel, the musical programme began. White floor cloths were laid out, the glitter of the silver *paandaan* and *khaasdaan* was blinding, as was the sparkle of the crystal chandelier. Well-known classical singers and dancers graced the occasion with their presence. Acchan

Maharaj's ankle bells created such magic that I was dazed and could no longer think.

Around this time my engagement was broken and thus an important decision in my life, proved a failure.

NOTES

1. The mythical land of fairies (Lit: Caucasia).

✛ 9 ✛

WINTERS IN RAMPUR
1935–1940

Every year, Papa would come back from England in winter. After his return, the celebrations marking the birthdays of His Highness and Apa Jan, as well as the traditional Christmas parties, commenced. Nawab Raza Ali Khan, was very keen on western lifestyles, thought and culture. During his reign, Englishmen held posts in nearly every department at Rampur. The entertainment of the guests went on from November to January. Local Englishmen, along with other officials from abroad, were regular guests; special arrangements were made for their stay in Khasbagh Palace. During this time, well-organized hunting parties equipped with tents and provisions frequently set out on elephants, to hunt tigers.

Christmas carried its own special brand of appeal. Beautiful decorations graced the bungalows of the English. At the fancy dress parties for children, Father Christmas handed out gifts, and the festivities at night included a dinner and dance. On Christmas Eve and on New Year's Eve, a very elaborate *soiree* was held at Khasbagh Palace. The banquet table and the ballroom presented a picture of splendour, a fine reflection of the glory of the Rampur rulers.

❖ ❖ ❖

SOJOURN IN KASHMIR
1937–1940

Papa left for England in 1936 with Yusuf, who had been admitted to Pembroke College, Cambridge. That same year, Papa attended the coronation of King George VI in London. We were back in Mussoorie where the usual hustle and bustle prevailed. In the English shops, there was wonderful merchandize imported from England. The sales people were also English, so that a visit to these shops made one feel that one was in England.

In September we returned to Rampur and Papa came back from England in October. Piles of correspondence awaited him. One of the letters was from the Maharajah of Kashmir and contained a special request to join his Cabinet. Papa was very touched by the high regard in which the Maharajah held him and, after some reflection, he accepted the portfolio of Home Minister in Kashmir.

In April 1937, we left for Kashmir, accompanied by Papa and the household staff. The four years we spent there were filled with good times. What beautiful places we visited, what wondrous scenes we witnessed. Then, the Second World War broke out and the world was thrown into turmoil. Train travel became more and more difficult and Papa thought it best that we make plans to return to Rampur.

❖ ❖ ❖

MUSSOORIE AGAIN

In 1941, we went to Mussoorie for the summer with Papa and we went there again the following year. The month of July in Mussoorie is very pleasant. There is a pleasant breeze blowing everywhere and greenery abounds. One day there was heavy rain accompanied by lightning and thunder. Suddenly I heard that some guests had arrived, but when I came out of my room I didn't see anyone, except a man leaving in a raincoat. Bahan Fakhra informed me that he was Sonny Habibullah's brother, Isha'at, and had come to pay his respects to Papa. What a coincidence that the next day, my father's doctor and a close family friend, Dr Saeed Khan, invited us for tea and I met Isha'at there. It seems that our stars were drawn to each other. His friend and my cousin, Syed Enver Masood, the son of Sir Ross Masood, became instrumental in bringing us closer and our wedding date was set for 4 December 1942. Nawab Raza Ali Khan and Apa Jan also approved of the match and everyone else in the family too was delighted with this alliance.

❖ ❖ ❖

MY WEDDING
4 DECEMBER 1942

Since Papa was very ill, Nawab Raza Ali Khan took over the preparations for my wedding and made elaborate arrangements. On 4 December 1942, a train arrived in Rampur, shimmering in the rays of the rising sun and brought the *baraat,* the bridegroom and his family from Lucknow. They arrived in great style, with all the men, including the bridegroom, dressed in brocade *sherwanis.* They were received with garlands of gold strands and flowers. Among them was Isha'at's eldest brother, Ali Bahadur 'Sonny' Habibullah, his nephew, Chaudhry Anwar Ali, his uncle, Syed Shahabuddin Kirmani, and his cousins, Rishad Hussain Kidwai and Maulana Jamal Mian of Firangi Mahal. His friends included Raja Sahib

Mahmudabad, Raja Sahib Pirpur, Kanwar Surat Bahadur Shah, Nawab Muzaffar Ali Qizilbash, Syed Enver Masood and his brother, Syed Akbar Masood.

Everyone was taken to Khasbagh Palace. After refreshments, the *begumaat* changed into their formal clothes and were received by the ladies of my family in the *zenana* at Rosaville. They were a beautiful sight, all of them in their fine jewellery and their trailing *farshi pyjamas* of different designs and colours, swirling around. They filled the *zenana* with gaiety. Sultana Akbar Masood, was there as a special guest, and looked beautiful in a silvery blue saree. They were taken to the *mehfil khana* and the *mirasans* started singing:

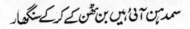

The in-laws come dressed up in their best finery.

In the *mehfil khana*, a special seating area was set up for the in-laws. There were brocade bolsters and *masnads* spread on the *chandni*; the guests were presented with fragrant garlands, scent, sweet drinks and specially prepared *paans* served in silver *khasdaans*, while the *mirasans* continued to sing. The guests included the bridegroom's mother, Begum Inam Habibullah, her daughters-in-law, Attia and Hamida Habibullah and Qaisra Anwar Ali and her niece, Soraya Abbasi.

While the festivities continued outside, I was being dressed up in my wedding clothes. There was a flurry of activity when Apa Jan appeared and proceeded to give instructions: all the accessories needed for my adornment were ready within minutes. I was conscious of the commotion all around. Someone removed the *dullai* from my head; another lady placed a red silk handkerchief to veil my face; a voice asked for the gold and red silken strands to prepare a *mobaf* for braiding my hair; a vial containing the *itr* of *chambeli* was opened. Pleating the hair, takes a very long time. A silver pencil is used to make a centre parting and the hair is pulled back, leaving two curls on either side of the face. The hair is then dabbed with a type of glue—*bedana*—in a pouch, then with sandal paste and covered with a sprinkling of glittering *afshaan*. On the other side of the room, married women sprinkled special bridal fragrances on my wedding robes. From the rooms beyond, echoed the voices of the *mirasans*.

My *reet ka jora*, the wedding robes, consisted of a matching, *karchobi kurta* and *orhni*, and a matching *farshi pyjama* culminating in a *giloree go't*, a fine, multi-coloured patchwork of triangles. After my jewellery was in place, my *ghungat* was arranged with a special veil called *maqna*. Some of the ladies led me to the *mehfil khana* for the ceremony of the *arsi mus'haf*. There was a sudden excitement as the bridegroom entered the *zenana*. His cousins and sisters-in-law hastened towards him with the corner of a *ganga-jamni dupatta*, which they held on his head, for luck. They brought him to the *masnad*, where I was seated. He looked very handsome in his *zarbaft sherwani*. His face was curtained with the golden strands of *sehra*, covered by another of flowers, while a garland of flowers hung from his neck. In his hand he clutched a red silken handkerchief. The *mirasans* broke into a song.

Later as I was leaving for Lucknow with my new family, I was very sad and tearful at the thought of being separated from my ailing father. Unfortunately, that was the last time I was to see him.

When the *baraat* arrived in Lucknow, Isha'at's younger sister, Tazeen, was the first to receive me. She had not come to Rampur because it was not the custom for an unmarried girl to leave her home to mingle with a stranger's family. She and her cousins began to tease Isha'at and would not let him enter the house, until he gave them their *naig,* a gift of money. This was finally presented to them by Mummy, my mother-in-law, amid much laughter and banter. Then they took me inside. In accordance to an old custom, Isha'at had to touch my feet with strands of green grass soaked in milk. A *milad* was recited. I went inside to pay my respects to Abbajan, my father-in-law (Sheikh Mohammed Habibullah, Taluqdar of Saidanpur) who placed his hand on my head, as a blessing. After two or three days, preparations were made to present me to the *begumaat* of Lucknow.

A huge marquee was set up in the big lawn adjacent to the bungalow and it was heavily decorated with floral motifs. This *mehfil khana,* which was for women only, was furnished with *chandni* and scattered with *masnads* and brocade bolsters. Silver *khaasdaans* to serve *paan* were placed in rows. In the middle of the room was the velvet *masnad,* decorated with beautiful gold embroidery, on which I was to sit. The gathering of ranis, maharanis, and other *begumaat,* all of them extremely well-dressed, graceful, of regal bearing and well-spoken, conjured up images of the court of Oudh.

I was dressed up again in a new bridal outfit, for this occasion. Now I was wearing a *farshi pyjama* with a wavy, multi-coloured *aab-e-leher* border, a waisted, long sleeved, pomegranate-red jacket or *shaluka,* and a heavily embroidered *badla ki orhni.* Accompanied by my sister-in-law, Hamida Bhabi, I entered the *mehfil khana.* The moment I set foot on the *masnad* the *mirasans* broke into songs of felicitations. The *begumaat* were all anxious to see me. Hamida Bhabi slowly lifted my veil and I heard someone say to my mother-in-law, 'Begum Habibullah have you selected all three of your daughters-in-law from *Koh Qaf?*'

There was no *purdah* at our wedding reception. A few days later, I stood next to Isha'at, wearing a saree of gold tissue. The presence of the Governor, Sir

Morris Hallet and his wife, Lady Hallet, was considered nothing less than a royal event. The *taluqdaars* of Lucknow, rajas, maharajahs, nawabs, nobles, friends, and relatives, all were invited. Isha'at's father was very fond of chrysanthemums and every year he won the award for the best chrysanthemums in Lucknow. There was just a little chill in the air since it was the beginning of winter, the flowers were in full bloom and, walking through the garden with Isha'at's father, Sir Morris complimented him on the beautiful flowers.

چمن آتش گل سے دہکا ہوا   ہوا کے سبب باغ مہکا ہوا
چمن سے بھرا باغ گل سے چمن   کہیں نرگس و گل کہیں یاسمن
کہیں جعفری اور گیندا کہیں   سماں شب کے داؤ دلیوں کا کہیں

The garden is ablaze with the fire of flowers,
The air has endowed the garden with fragrance,
The garden is bursting with flowers, flowers fill the garden.

✥ 10 ✥

WEDDING CEREMONIES AND MUSICAL ASSEMBLIES

In those days wedding ceremonies and wedding rituals went on for several days in a row. Life was very comfortable, there were no pressures and everything was easily available. All one had to do was to give an order. The *mughalanis* were usually busy with stitching and embroidering garments for years prior to the actual wedding. When the happy day arrived, family members assembled, and young girls, dressed in glittering clothes, presented a picture of colourful festivity. The hall would be crowded with guests and a bevy of servants would be running about taking care of this and that while the voices of the *mirasans* singing echoed everywhere.

✥ ✥ ✥

THE ENGAGEMENT CEREMONY

All the women in the household joined in the preparation of the bride's dress, a *gharara*-suit tastefully and elegantly embroidered in gold and silver thread. The *imam zamin* was either red or green, and was heavily ornamented with a gold *mohar* sewn into it. The trays were decorated with red twill with a shiny edging; the coverings for the trays were even more elaborate. Young girls, dressed in colourful, glittering clothes, carried these trays and arrived in a procession at the bride's house, singing together as they approached. In the tray would be a ring set in precious stones, an *imam zamin,* the bride's engagement dress, colourful glass bangles, and *misri.* In another tray there would be a *teeka,* bracelets, necklace, earrings for the bride, all made from white, scented *motia* and *bela* flowers and touches of tinsel.

The bride's friends brought her out and made her sit on the *masnad.* First, the *imam zamin,* was tied, which is symbolic of entrusting the bride to the care of Imam Raza *Aleh-his-Salam.* Then the whole assembly would resound with the echo of the *dholak* and the singing would begin. The married women would deck the bride with the floral ornaments, the ring would be placed on her finger, a *misri* would be placed in her mouth and after that, money would be waved over her head to be later given away in charity as a good omen. Congratulations and good wishes would echo in the room.

❖ ❖ ❖

PRE-WEDDING CELEBRATIONS

Naubat Chapai

The wedding celebrations were announced by the playing of the *naubat.* The men gathered in the men's chambers as part of an auspicious ritual. The brothers and brothers-in-law of the bride were invited to inaugurate the ceremony by dipping their hands into a silver bowl of sandal paste. Then they touched the *naqara* or drum lightly, in turn, to give it a tap and the *naubat nawaz* picked up the sound and started playing immediately. The brothers and brothers-in-law were presented with a gift signifying good luck, in the form of cash enclosed in *zari* bags. It was customary to decorate the *naubat khana* with tinsel and red twill.

Dhol Chapai

The following day, women guests began arriving in the *zenana mehfil khana*. There was a lot of hustle bustle. Dressed in beautiful, glittering attire, the sisters of the groom entered the *mehfil khana* where the *masnad* and cushions decorated with *kalabattun,* awaited them. The *mirasans,* in *lachka* and *zari peshwazes,* were ready to sing. The *dholak,* encased in a *benarsi* cover with colourful cords stretched tightly over it, was in tune. The sisters dipped their fingers in sandal paste and then proceeded to tap the *dholak* lightly. The *mirasans* immediately picked up the beat and began singing. The festive mood of the wedding was in full swing now. The gifts of cash and clothing for the sisters were arranged decoratively in silver trays.

Rang

This beautiful and lively ceremony was conducted before the wedding day. Red, yellow, and green dyes in the water fountain created an image of the rainbow. Young girls teased each other and played *rang* by squirting coloured dyes through a spray gun. The burst of colour and the spirit of merriment that prevailed set a happy mood for the wedding. The songs of the *mirasans* created a festive air.

Sehnak

This was a *niaz* carried out in the name of Hazrat Fatima, the Prophet's (PBUH) daughter. A holy observance, it took place before the wedding. A tablecloth was set up for the *niaz* and, *Sayidanis* offered prayers over sweet rice arranged in big, low, earthen bowls called *koondas* and a suit of clothes and bangles placed next to them. After this sanctified ceremony, the fabric for the bride's wedding suit was measured out for cutting and stitching.

Ma'yun

The ceremony of *ma'yun*, also called *manjha*, was made performed at the bride's house. *Ubtan* to beautify and massage the bride afterwards was made, and delicious round *peendis* were prepared in the house. A corner of the room, where the bride would sit, was decorated especially for the occasion. Yellow curtains, yellow covering for the *masnad*, yellow cushions, all edged with silver, created a special allure. The bride's yellow suit and the attractive surroundings enhanced the bride's simple, unadorned appearance. At the time of the ceremony, the bride was seated on a low silver stool; a green *paan* leaf covered her upturned palm and *ubtan* and *peendis* were placed on it. She was also given a bite of the *peendi* as a good omen after which a *kangna*, a glittering, multi-coloured cord, with a *karchob* flower, was tied on her wrist. Following this, coins were showered on her for good luck and the *mirasans* started the singing again.

Mehndi

This ceremony usually took place on the fourth day after the *manjah*. The bridegroom, friends, relatives and guests brought the bride's *mehndi* with great pomp and ceremony. The items included were *suhag pura*, floral ornaments, six or seven types of dried fruit, an old coconut, two *paans*, *afshaan*, glass bangles, *misri*, and a decorated tray of *mehndi*. The *mehndi* was embellished with designs of flowers and leaves made with *go'ta* and *afshaan*. Then the candles were arranged all around the *mehndi* and lit—the scene was breathtaking. Rows of young girls, dressed in glittering attire, their anklets jingling, appeared daintily and gracefully with the trays, the ornamented tray covers too were a dazzling sight.

Surrounded by her close friends, the bride sat on the *masnad*. The married women performed the rituals to ensure good omens. They decked the bride with floral ornaments, applied sandal paste, *itr* and *afshaan* in her parting, placed a *paan* in each of her hands, and then applied *mehndi* and *ubtan* on her palms, which were kept one on top of the other. After this the bride was given a bite of *misri* and the ritual of *godh bharai* was performed by placing fruits, nuts and a coconut in the bride's lap while money was showered over her. The bride's sisters started singing in their melodious voices.

❖ ❖ ❖

THE WEDDING DAY

The wedding day finally arrived, in fulfillment of so many hopes, expectations, prayers and vows. The *naubat* was sounded and the wedding became a reality. Guests thronged the *mehfil khana* and the sound of the *mirasans* singing in the *zenana* echoed everywhere. In the *mardana*, the bridegroom looked magnificent as he sat on the brocade *masnad*. He wore a golden *kemkhab sherwani* and a *zari* turban decorated with a *turah*. The elders of the family performed the *sehra-bandhni*, veiling the bridegroom's face with two *sehra's*, one of glittering *go'ta* and the other, covering it, of white flowers and delicate tinsel. The bride's *nikah* was performed in the *zenana*, with her brothers and uncles acting as the four witnesses and then conveying her assent to the bridegroom in the *mardana*. After the *nikah*, the room resounded with congratulations. Dried dates, called *chu'haras* and round balls of puffed sugar, called *nuquals* were distributed to the guests. The singers broke into *raag durbari*.

Arsi mus'haf

After the *nikah* the women of the family helped the bride to dress. She wore the *reet ka jora*, fragrant with a scent, *itr-e-suhag*, presented by her in-laws; then she put on the jewellery, they had given. Her *nath* and the *teeka* shone brilliantly and, shrouded by a fine, transparent red veil, *maqna*, she seemed ethereal. The bridegroom's sisters and sisters-in-law, stretched a *ganga-jamini* dupatta over his head and led him into the *zenana*. He was seated cross-legged, opposite the bride, on the *masnad*. Between them, a mirror edged with embossed silver was placed on top of the Quran, which had been opened at *sura Akhlas*. A big, red *karchob dupatta* was thrown over, to cover the couple. The *sura Yusuf* was recited to bless them. The groom had to persuade the bride to open her eyes and both saw each other, for the first time, reflected in the mirror.

Rukhsati

The departure of the bride from her parents' house was a difficult time indeed. The custom was that her brothers were called into the *zenana*. Into each corner of her *dupatta* they knotted betel nuts, a rupee, green blades of grass, whole turmeric, saying as they did so, 'Sister, I tie your virtue with this knot.' Amir Khusro has written many sad songs especially for this occasion. Everyone was moved to tears when the *mirasans* sang:

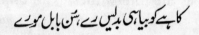

Why did you wed me so far away from home, my father?

❖ ❖ ❖

THE ARRIVAL OF THE BRIDE AT THE BRIDEGROOM'S HOME

What splendour and ceremony accompanied a *baraat* when it returned home with the bride! The guests crowded the house, the groom's sisters ran about in their shimmering finery, the sound of the *mirasans* singing, echoed everywhere.

The bride, accompanied by the groom, was escorted in by his sisters and seated on the *masnad*. The bridegroom had to symbolically wash his bride's feet with milk. A silver basin, a silver jug and, a silver soap dish containing some blades of grass, soaked in milk, were placed nearby. The bridegroom touched the bride's feet with the grass for good fortune. This was followed by a ceremony in which small portions of *kheer* were placed in the palm of the groom and bride, to be fed to the other. Finally the bride was presented to all the guests, a custom called *ru'numai*.

Chauthi

This was a ceremony, performed at the home of the bride's parents, when she and the groom visited them the following day. Fruit and vegetables were arranged

57. A princess of Rampur in traditional bridal jewellery. She is wearing *jhoomar* in her hair which has splayed strings of pearls, linked at each end by ornaments of precious stones, the lower culminating with bunches of small pearls, resting on the forehead. The *teeka* is set with a large stone in the centre, surrounded by other precious stones edged with graded drop pearls. The *nath* in her nose has a large pair of pearls with a ruby in between. Her ears are covered by pearl *goshwaras* attached to her hair and her *jhumka* earrings. There is usually a large solitaire pearl below the *jhumkas* to create a balance.

58. A princess of Rampur wearing traditional cosmetics. In her hair, she has marked out a pattern of squares with *bedana*, sprinkled with sandalwood and glitter. She has also applied glitter in the parting, as well as the edge of her hair outlining the forehead and on her eyelids and cheeks. She has applied *bedana* to hold the sequins following the curve of her eyebrows. Her lips are outlined with black *missi* and she has eaten a *paan*, a betel leaf, to give a reddish tint in the centre, with its juice.

59. The *samdhans,* ladies of the bridegroom's family, line up to go with the *baraat* to the bride's home. On the extreme right, Kishwar Yusuf Khan wears an *orhni* belonging to her mother-in-law, Lady Abdus Samad Khan, embroidered in 1913 by Haji Ali Jan in Old Delhi with *karchob* work on a net *dupatta.*

60. A bridegroom veiled by a *sehra*, led in by his sisters.

61. A bride's face covered by a *maqna,* a diaphanous red veil of organza with tinsel stripes.

decoratively in a tray, with intertwined flowers rolled or shaped into sticks and eight small balls. The bride and groom, seated cross-legged on the *masnad*, played a game, the *chauthi*, flicking the balls and a *kangana* of flowers to each other over a silver bowl, filled with water. The rule was that neither the ball nor the *kangana* could fall into the bowl. The *mirasans* supervised the game and sang:

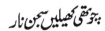

Playing chauthi with my beloved.

Nawab Raza Ali Khan too has composed one of the most beautiful of songs about the playing of the *chauthi*.

Juta Chupai or Hiding the Shoe

In this ceremony, the bride's sisters, cousins and women friends hid the groom's shoe, amid much laughter and teasing, so that he couldn't leave. The shoe was only returned after much negotiation and a gift of money from him, to be distributed among the young girls.

❖ ❖ ❖

SEHRA

These are verses written for a wedding and in Rampur, were usually composed by the court poet. Apa Jan wrote her own compositions however, and had such a profound knowledge of literature, that she wrote a *sehra* for the wedding of my youngest brother, General Sahibzada Mohammad Yaqub Khan to Tuba Khaleeli, in Karachi.

خوش انداز سہرا خوش اسلوب سہرا   مبارک ہو اے مہربانی یعقوب سہرا

سراسر تصور کی تصویر نکلا   ہے ویسا ہی جیسا تھا مطلوب سہرا

کھلے بعد مدت کے گلہائے ارماں   نہ کیوں ہو رضا ہم کو محبوب سہرا

نہ ہے عزم منزل کہ جب تک نہ پہنچا   دکھا تا رہا صبر ایوب سہرا

گلوں سے گلستان کو ہے جتنی عزت   ہمیں بھی ہے اتنا ہی مرغوب سہرا

Such a beautiful sehra, such an elegant sehra
For Brother Yaqub blessed be this sehra.
It is as we had imagined it,
Shaped like our desires the sehra.
Our hopes have blossomed after a lifetime,
Why, Raza, should we not love the sehra.
Until it did not attain its destination
A reflection it revealed of patience, the sehra.
Just as the garden adores its flowers,
So we cherish and love the sehra.

✢ 11 ✢

THE OBSERVANCES OF MUHARRAM
AT THE COURT OF NAWAB RAZA ALI KHAN

شبیہ امام زماں کھینچتے ہیں
تصور میں تصویر جاں کھینچتے ہیں

We create the pictures of the Imam of the times,
In our minds we create the picture of one who is loved.

The moment the new moon of Muharram was sighted
a melancholy enveloped everyone and the events of
Karbala took shape before our eyes. My parents
observed Muharram for twelve days. Music and singing
were prohibited and we were expected to dress simply
and not attend any ceremony or celebration during
this time. *Nazr* and *niaz* were carried out. On the
seventh of Muharram, a *nazr* was made with milk and,
at this time, my mother would read the *Shahadatnama*,
the story of Imam Hussain's martyrdom. My sister and
I sat next to my mother, our heads covered in green
dupattas, and listened attentively to the accounts of
the Imam's martyrdom. Here is a verse from the
Shahadatnama:

بزمِ جہاں میں دھوم ہے ماتمِ محسین کی

یارو یہ غم فزا ہے شہادتِ حسین کی

*The world echoes with the mourning of Hussain's
    martyrdom,*
Friends, this martyrdom wrenches one's heart with anguish.

کیا کوئی سمجھے مومنو رتبہ حسین کا

فرماتے ہر گھڑی تھے یہ محبوبِ کبریا

*Good people, how can anyone understand Hussain's status
Says this beloved of God every minute.*

On the tenth day of Muharram, the Ashura, guests
arrived in the *mardana* for the breaking of the fast.
Khichra was cooked especially for this day and
afterwards *nazr* portions were handed out to everyone.

The rulers of Rampur belonged to the Fiqah-e-
Jaffria. The traditions once observed during
Muharram by the royal house of Oudh, were reflected
at the court at Rampur as well and were carried out
with the same seriousness, veneration, and ceremonial.
The entire State was plunged into mourning. Food
was distributed to the poor and the portions prepared
for the *majlis* ran into the hundreds: a huge tray with
portions would arrive at our house as well. *Dhania* and
go'ta, a mixture of roasted almonds and coriander
seed, coconut pieces, aniseed, cardamom and betel
nuts, were placed in white cotton bags and were
distributed widely, but at the *majlis* itself, the *dhania*
and *go'ta* were given to the ladies in small, beautiful
batwas or pouches. During the period of mourning,
this was consumed instead of the usual *paan*.

Relatives travelled great distances to be in Rampur
to observe Muharram. Ammajan said that some guests

had come from Nawab Mustafa Khan Shefta's family home, Mustafa Castle in Meerut; Agha Jan Sahib's family had come from Sehswan, and Abdullah Khan had travelled from Jansath. *Marsia* reciters, people who recited *soz*, and special *maulanas* were invited from Lucknow to address the *majlis*. Separate *majlis* were held for men and women every day. The name of Imam Hussain was the only name to be heard everywhere in the Qila. The rulers of Rampur held such strong beliefs that they would not allow any other subject besides the martyrdom at Karbala to preoccupy them during the period of mourning.

On the seventh of Muharram the *mehndi* was taken out in a procession, which, replete with ceremonial sobriety, passed in front of our house for hours. The whole effect was one of great sadness. The soldiers, wearing black armbands, marched solemnly with their guns lowered and facing down, a *zamburchi* rode a camel, a drummer sitting on a horse with a black saddle beat a drone, while the participants, beating their chests to the rhythms of the *tashey* and the *dhol*, chanted:

مہندی آئی ہے قاسم بنّے کی

It's the mehndi of Qasim, the bridegroom, that we bring.

The English bandmaster, Mr Curtis and the English photographer, Mr Mitchell, both wearing black suits, took part in the ceremonial chest-beating and recited '*Wai Muhammada, Kushta shud Hussain!*' (Alas, Muhammad, Hussain is killed!), to the best of their ability. Attired in green clothing, men carried decorated shrubs and earthen pots filled with dried fruit on their heads. The *mehndi* was adorned in trays with mica and flowers. The recitations were heart-rending.

On the ninth day of Muharram the procession carrying the *tazia*s walked through the streets. Some of these *tazias*, each an intricately wrought replica of the mausoleums of Imam Hussain and Imam Hassan, were so heavy that six or seven men together carried them on their shoulders during the long walk. On the night of the ninth, everyone stayed awake and on the morning of the tenth of Muharram, the *tazias* were taken out to a ground embodying Karbala and buried symbolically until the next year.

During Muharram, stalls, called *sabils*, were set up at every step to provide water and sweetened milk to the members of the procession. *Nazr* and *niaz* were an every-day event. The *imambara* was incomparably beautiful and a sight to behold: it contained *karchobi* banners, gold *alams*, some studded with precious stones. Rows of silver *tazias*, each dedicated to a member of the royal family, glistened brilliantly; the *ganga-jamini* latticework on the *minbar*, the pulpit, was of such exquisite workmanship, that it sparkled under the light of the chandelier.

The commemoration of the events at Karbala is no less than a miracle. It has been more than thirteen hundred years, but the tenth of Muharram brings with it the same lamentation and sorrow. Today, on that day, we can still visualize the hell let loose at Karbala; for the atrocities that were committed there against the person of Hazrat Imam Hussain, along with the other martyrs of Karbala, presented to the world an example of supreme sacrifice. There is no one who hasn't been shaken by this event. Birds and animals too are trembling, the heavens and the earth cry out 'God, Protect us! Protect us!'

My pen too concedes now and is tearful:

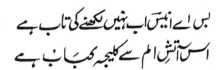

O Anis! I can no longer write,
Enough, my heart burns with the fire of grief.

❖ ❖ ❖

THE ROYAL TABLES AT
THE COURT OF RAMPUR

With the onset of turbulent times, during the reign of
Wajid Ali Shah and the War of Independence in 1857,
destruction descended on Lucknow. Artists and writers
fled to take refuge in Rampur. Famous poets, writers,
religious scholars, *marsia* reciters, storytellers and
musicians arrived in droves. The rulers of Rampur
gathered them together as if they were precious pearls
and extended them every courtesy and honour
imaginable. As a result, Rampur, though a small state,
acquired great fame for its culture and its patronage
of the arts.

Along with other things, Rampur's menus were also
famous all over Hindustan. The chefs here were
superb craftsmen and each had his designated skill.
For example, a *qaliya* master, was in charge of preparing different types of *qaliya*, a curry which had specific
spices as its base. Then there was a different specialist
in rice dishes. The *kababis* made only *kababs*, while the
experts in desserts such as *halwas* were without parallel.
Some of the dishes prepared in Rampur were as
follows:

Qaliya

The two main curries served in Rampur were the *qaliya* and the *qorma*. The former contains turmeric; the later is made with coriander. The *qaliyas* were of various types, namely *kundan qaliya, rattan qaliya, qaliya with almonds, pasandey ka qaliya, koftey ka qaliya,* chicken *qaliya.* There was one special *qaliya* with white chicken in which milk, yoghurt and green chillies are used as the main ingredients. Another was *qaliya taar* the favourite dish of Rampur, which is made of the finest beef and its fat, cooked in so much *ghee,* that when it is eaten, the *ghee* drips through your fingers in strands.

Shab degh is a Mughal dish, a *qaliya* which takes hours to cook overnight; it is very rich because the gravy has the stock of mutton chops; the *koftas* are prepared separately and added to it; also added are whole turnips pierced and filled with *gur,* or raw sugar, lightly fried with turmeric. Both the *koftas* and turnips are then added to the curry and the whole is cooked on a slow fire with a dash of saffron and *kewra.* This is a different variety to the famous Kashmiri *shab degh.*

Rice

Some of the *pulao* dishes are: *dam pukht pulao,* with whole partridge, or quails or whole leg of mutton; *pathani pulao* cooked with mutton chops; *yakhni pulao,* made of rice and mutton stock. Then there is quail *biryani,* and a host of other *biryani* dishes, including *biryani parcha,* made from the rib of mutton. The difference between a *pulao* and a *biryani* is that in the latter, the meat is first prepared as a *qorma* curry, then mixed with the half done rice and sprinkled with saffron and *kewra* and cooked very slowly.

Sweet Rice

There are many different varieties of sweet rice, served as a dessert.

The *muttanjan,* has a sweet and sour flavour and is the most difficult to cook; it contains sugar which is four times the weight of the uncooked rice and is garnished with tiny, round, sweet *gulab jamans* and tiny, round, spicy mutton *koftas,* used to decorate the rice. Saffron is used in large quantities in this recipe.

The *muza'ffir* uses half the quantity of sugar than the *muttanjan* but it is very tasty because there is a syrupy fruit preserve, a *murabba* of apples, or pears or *karaunda* added to it. *Zarda* is not as rich; it uses much less *ghee* and sugar but it is very tasty, and is garnished with raisins and nuts.

Safaida is a sweet rice which is very difficult to prepare, as it absorbs five times the amount of sugar; it has no saffron and its beauty is that the sugar and *ghee* are absorbed totally. Each grain stands out separately and is so white that the sugary syrup coating has the sheen of diamonds.

Other varieties of sweet rice include *bhuna meetha chawwal*—sautéed rice, rice with sugar cane juice and *ghee, rab ke chawwal, gur ke chawwal, khoey ke chawwal.*

Anar or pomegranate *pulao* consists of white, sweet rice, laid out in a silver bowl, called a *qaab.* In each *qaab,* there are four pomegranates, crafted from sugar and red food colouring. These are so lifelike, that they appear to have been freshly picked. Inside, there are tiny seeds, fashioned from slivered almonds and enmeshed in a pitted skin made of green *petha,* a transparent pumpkin sweetmeat.

For *angur* or grape *pulao,* life-like grapes are made from green *petha* and arranged in bunches on the sweet rice. There is also a *ananas* or pineapple *pulao* with a life-size pineapple fashioned from sugar and food colour and displayed whole with sweet white rice, on each *qaab*, or silver plate.

Varieties of Kababs

These are a great speciality made from meat, fish or poultry. A particular speciality is called *kabab urus-e behri*, made of *sanwal*, a freshwater fish. This requires many seers of fish, to be made into a fish shaped *kabab*, two feet long and quite wide. The scales have a different flavour, the tongue has a different taste, as does the tail. This is served on a silver tray and so reconstructed that it looks like a whole fish, straight from the river.

Other *kabab* recipes include *kabab-e murg-e mussallam, kabab-e seekh, kabab-e nargisi, ganderi-daar, shaami kabab, kache gosht ke kabab, gole ke kabab*, and *babari kabab*.

Halwas and Sweets

There were very many different types of *halwas* and sweets in Rampur which are seldom seen anymore. Some of these are:

Dar-e-bahisht (gateway to Paradise), a flaky sweet made of crushed almonds or pistachios, *ghee* and sugar and cut into squares when set. *Qumaq* is a kind of *samosa* made of flan pastry, filled with nuts and dipped in syrup, which dries on the sweet before it is served. *Pari qurmay* is a round or oval pastry made of flour and filled with nuts, coated with sugar. *Nan-e-santara* is a sweet made of orange peel, orange juice, *ghee*, sugar and shaped into flat thin rounds, like a *roti*. *Shahkh-e-tallai*, is another *roti*-shaped sweet, made of saffron and sugar and golden in colour. *Khase-key-ladoo*, are very similar to normal gram flour *ladoos* available today, but they are much, much larger, about a quarter pound each and the gram flour is mixed with ground pistachios, almonds and whole raisins.

Loz-e-Jehangiri, named after the Emperor Jahangir, this diamond shaped sweetmeat is made from almonds, *ghee, khoya,* and sugar and is very delicious, with layers of crushed pistachios.

There are many varieties of *halwas*, each made by cooking a fruit, or a vegetable or eggs, or nuts or dates, with sugar, *ghee,* milk and/or cream for several hours. *Halwa sohn*, which is made of wheat and can still be found today, is the most difficult to make and is the king of *halwas*.

Satoris and *peendis* are also special sweets, made of semolina, almonds, nuts, *makkana*, coconuts, pistachios, *ghee* and sugar. *Satori* is soft and served in a bowl; *peendis* are made into rounds like very large *ladoos* and presented on ceremonial occasions.

Namish is a great delicacy, made by collecting layers and layers of froth from sweet milk and then leaving it outside in the cool dew overnight, to set; it is eaten with a crisp, very thin *roti* which has a biscuit-like flavour.

Puris of cream are made of clotted cream, collected layer upon layer to form a cake and served with sugar.

Rampur's *gulathi* is very famous, very rich and very delicious. Rice is cooked in milk for a long time, mixed with *khoya* and sugar and smoked with charcoal. When a brown layer, *khurchan*, forms at the bottom of the dish, it is removed, scraped and cut into round shapes and used to garnish the *gulathi*.

❖ ❖ ❖

THE ETIQUETTE OF THE PAANDAAN

In our culture the *paandaan*, the casket for betel leaves, betel nuts and other accoutrements has a special ritual and, together with the *ugaldaan* or spitoon, is a decorative item in every house. A warm welcome for every guest begins with an offering of the *paan*. A *giloree*, a rolled up, triangular *paan*, is presented in a *khaasdaan* and the person receiving it acknowledges the offer with respectful salutations. Hyderabad Deccan has been the centre of our culture for centuries and in many parts of Hyderabad age-old traditions and ceremonies are still in practice. There, guests are also offered *paan* when leaving.

When a *paandan* is carried into a gathering, it is placed in front of the hostess and is a sight worth seeing. The silver *paandan* is covered with a glittering gold, *banarsi* cover, a *qasma*, edged with a *paraqa* border and embellished further with gold *kiran* and *banat*.

Paans are of many different varieties, namely, *saanchi, bangla, desi, kapuri* etc. Dark red *katha* and white *chuna* are prepared with the utmost care and are served so fresh, that the mere sight of these in the *paandaan's* small pots, increases the desire for *paan*, even before they are applied to it, with tiny silver spatulas. *Chhalia*, betel nuts, cut finely in tiny squares and tiny cardamoms encased in silver paper, are a beautiful sight indeed; while minute, fragrant balls of *qiwwam*, or tobacco wrapped in silver leaf, create a special effect and act as natural breath fresheners. The design of a *paandaan, khaasdaan* and *ugaldaan* differ from area to area, each marked by its own characteristic embellishment and motifs. Those with the latticed designs are a specialty of Hyderabad. The *nagardaan* is a small box, in the shape of a *paan*, in which the *paans* are arranged for the guests.

The etiquette of the *paandaan* involves a ceremonious ritual of politeness and respect. The hostess presents the *giloree* rolled in silver leaf and placed in the *khaasdaan,* to her guest. Picking up the *giloree,* the guest raises a hand to the forehead in a respectful *ada'ab* of acknowledgement; the hostess also lowers her head once slightly in response.

What a fine sight *paan*s, coated with silver leaf and arranged in a silver tray, present at weddings and other such celebrations. It is known that the black *missi* on the teeth and the red of *paan* on the lips, were once considered integral to the adornment of women. Poets too have spoken lyrically of the *paan.*

✛ 12 ✛

THE INVESTITURE OF HIS HIGHNESS
NAWAB RAZA ALI KHAN,
AS THE RULER OF RAMPUR
HAMID MANZIL
1930

Morning dawned with a smile. The rays of the sun filled the hearts of people with gladness. This was that blessed day that everyone had been waiting for. In the Qila-e-Mualla, the festivity was reminiscent of a wedding. The melodious sound of the *naubat* echoed in the air, orders and injunctions were issued; a flurry of activity commenced in the state. Lords and noblemen and members of the royal staff took up their various duties. The army and the guard, with all their gear and their artillery, stood to attention.

Hamid Manzil is an impressive building; its gold dome and minarets and a wide, grand staircase, leading up to the entrance enhance its beauty. On this day, those stairs had been covered with a red baize carpet; on either side, stood lancers in red uniforms with glittering buttons. They had coloured turbans set smartly on their heads, stylish *kammarbunds* around the waist, and they stood like statues, holding silver spears in their white-gloved hands. At the foot of the staircase, were rows of elephants, on either side. They were heavily laden with gold and silver ornaments; their saddles were decorated with gold embroidery. Their *mahouts* seated in the *hawda* and dressed in a red baize uniform, awaited the arrival of His Highness. As soon as he appeared, all the elephants would present a salute by raising their trunks.

Inside, the walls and ceiling of the *durbar* hall, were decorated with intricate motifs in gold leaf. A large, dazzling cut-glass chandelier cascaded from the ceiling. An awning shot with gold thread, with a *kalabattun* fringe all around, and resting on four golden poles, had been set up on a raised platform. Each corner was decorated with a golden globe. Beneath the *kalabattun* was a *masnad* with a golden chair with a gold lion's head carved at the end of each arm and the Rampur crest at the back; it was upholstered in red velvet. Nearby there was a type of *hukkah*—a gold *pehchwan*—to complete the setting. Two attendants, attired in red uniforms with gold embroidery and wearing golden turbans, stood by the chair. One, held a golden fan; the other, a golden *chanwar*, or fly whisk.

A description of the court dress: a golden silk turban, a gold brocade sherwani and white *churidar* pyjama, a *benarsi patka* on the waist, studded belt, a sword with a gold hilt, green velvet scabbard, a pink silken handkerchief tied to the hilt, and all the official medals displayed.

On the right of the throne, sat the rulers of various princely states. The members of the Rampur royal family, noblemen, high-ranking army officials and aristocrats were on the left. The jewels of the ruling princes—the *kalghi* (aigrette), *tauq* (broad jewelled necklaces), *chandan haar* (long necklace) and *mala-i-marwardi* (strings of pearls) were without parallel.

Suddenly the gun salute was fired, creating a commotion. News arrived that the procession was about to enter the Hamid Gate entranceway. People thronged the area, the crowds thickened with each passing minute. The procession consisted of elephants, in turn carrying the *naubat* of four musician—with *naqara, shehnai,* flute and trumpet—the *naqeeb* or heralds, and the *mahi maratab.* The last was denoted with the figure of a fish with other insignia carried as ensigns upon elephants. Musicians played while carried by *kahars* on a platform called the *takht-i-roshan chauki;* singing girls performed on another, the *takht-i-haai tawafain.* They were followed by a brass band, the first and second infantry, the Gurkha band, the Gurkha Company, and golden carriages drawn by army horses. Finally, His Highness Nawab Raza Ali Khan, the new ruler of Rampur, made his appearance in his crown and coronation regalia. His carriage halted before Hamid Manzil. Elephants raised their trunks in salute. His Highness wearing a *tash badla* striped *sherwani* with jewelled buttons, rings on his fingers, and a *nau lakha* necklace studded with dazzling diamonds, gracefully ascended the stairs. The *chobdar,* or herald carrying a golden staff, walked ahead. At every step, to guide His Highness along, called out in a loud voice:

'*Nigah rubaru, gharib parwar, nawab salaamat.*'
'Behold! His Highness The Protector of The Poor! May He Be Blessed With a Long Life!'

When His Highness entered the *durbar* hall, the scene was that of incredible splendour. The musicians and singers struck up the *raag durbari* to the beat of the *tabla.* The festive song begun thus:

62. HH Nawab Raza Ali Khan of Rampur in his coronation regalia. His crown of diamonds and pearls forms the shape of a *topi* and the pear-shaped pearl at the top is part of a *kalghi* attached to it. There is a solitaire diamond in his left ear for good luck. His *sherwani* is of a green Benarsi *zari* brocade and has diamond buttons. His Cartier necklace which is part of the State Regalia has large diamonds which have a screw-like mechanism so that they can be easily removed. He is wearing a heart shaped marquise diamond in his left hand and a brilliant cut diamond in the right. The hilt of his sword and the scabbard are set in precious stones and he is sitting on a gold *Durbar* chair with a crown at the back and golden armrests.

63. HH Rafat Zamani Begum of Rampur.

ہمیشہ دلبر سبحاں مبارک باشد

الہی دولت و اقبال مبارک باشد

May you always be loved and blessed
May God always glorify you with riches and status.

Next, gold *ashrafis* were presented to His Highness,
in *nazr*. At that moment, the whole effect of the *durbar*,
the hall, the music filling the air, was that of a magical
fairyland. I could see everything clearly from the
upstairs gallery, on the second floor, where
arrangements had been made for Apa Jan and the
purdah ladies.

❖ ❖ ❖

THE MUSICAL TRADITION IN RAMPUR

An account by Nawab Raza Ali Khan[1]

'During the reign of my forefather, Nawab Yusuf Ali
Khan, the last of the Dagars[2] was Roshan Khan
Dagar, whose grave can still be found in Rampur.

'Basit Pyare Khan, the *rabab* player, Jaffar Khan
and Sadiq Ali, the singers, were at the court as well.
In the time of Nawab Kalb-e-Ali Khan, the singers
Khan Amir Khan, and Inaayat Khan performed at
the court while Mian Sayyed Shah, the *alghoza nawaz*,
gained repute as a musician. The flute player Wazir
Khan, the singer Nazir Khan, Fida Hussain the *sarod*
player, Gia Prashad the *pakhawaj* expert, Hussain
Ali Khan the *tabla* player, Hanif Khan the *sitar*
player, Kalka Binda Din who was a master of *kathak*,
Bhaya Ganpat Rao, Pandat Bhat Khanday, Thakur
Nawab Ali Khan, all renowned musicians, graced
the court of my father, Nawab Hamid Ali Khan. I

have put all these names together because these are pearls that have been gathered with great discernment by my forefathers.'

The Rampur *gharana* of music was famous. Nawab Raza Ali Khan followed in the footsteps of his ancestors. But, not only did he have superb performers at his court, he was an accomplished and talented musician himself. He wrote several books on music with *sangit sagar* notations and composed innumerable *raags* and *raagnian*. He was also a poet of Hindi. He set songs to *dhurpad, sadhra, hori, khayal, tarana, chitrang, tarwat, charbait,* wedding songs, and arranged *nohas* and *soz* to the accompaniment of special *raags* as well. He also played an excellent *pakhawaj* and *kher taal* (castanets). The world of music and song mourns his passing.

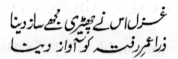

He has struck a ghazal, provide me an instrument,
Cry out for a moment for time gone by.

The masters whom I heard in Rampur were many: Ustaad Mushtaq Hussain Khan singing the *tarana* and *khayal*; Ustaad Ahmed Jan Khan Thirakwa, the *tabla nawaz*; Ustaad Sadiq Ali Khan, *beenkar*; Ustaad Hafiz Ali Khan, *sarod nawaz*; Sudeshri Bai, an accomplished singer of *tappa, thumri* and *nirat*; Ustaad Bare Ghulam Ali Khan whose singing of the *chaya* and *jejewanti* were without parallel; Ustaad Bundu Khan, *sarangi nawaz*, and his son Ustaad Umrao Khan whose *meg malhar* were especially memorable; Roshan Ara Begum, the consummate classical singer, Begum Akhtar, whose rendition of the *ghazal* was without equal; Ustaad Peyare Sahib Khan, who sang in a fine, melodious tenor; Acchan Maharaj, Birju Maharaj, Bechwa Jan, and Sitara Devi, all of whom were superb *kathak* dancers.

Listening to music at a recital or performance requires a certain etiquette. It is best to provide a seating arrangement on the floor and have only a few people in order to avoid using a microphone. The musician is the center of the *mehfil* and it is important for the listeners to maintain contact with the *ustaad*. They should remain silent and listen intently, breaking their silence only to offer praise in the form of '*Wah!Wah!*' or '*Mashallah! Mashallah!*' at the appropriate time during the performance.

❖ ❖ ❖

THE INVESTITURE OF APA JAN
AS HER HIGHNESS RAFAT ZAMANI BEGUM
ZENANA DURBAR
1930

The *zenana durbar* was held in Badshah Manzil, the Qila-e-Mualla's large *mahalsera*. The seating was arranged in the large hall. A white floor covering with colourful *masnads* and cushions was laid out. In the centre of the room a *karchobi* awning was set up on golden poles and all the four golden domes on the corners of the *namgira*, or awning, were of extraordinary craftsmanship. Under the awning was a *kalabattun masnad* and cushions of different sizes. On one side of the *masnad* was a gold *pehchwan* and on the other, gold *khasdaans* and *paandaans*. The *begumaat* of the royal family were seated on either side of the awning, beautifully dressed in *karchobi farshi pyjamas* and jewelled from head to toe. Other ladies were seated some distance away. The hall was aglitter with all their colourful attire, their shiny *dupattas* worked with gold and silver. In front of the *namgira* were groups of *mirasans,* who were all dressed in *karchobi peshwaz* and were waiting to perform. Bachwa Jan, the *kathak* maestro, wearing a *peshwaz* of golden tissue assumed a special pose as the leader, a few steps ahead of the *mirasans.*

After a while a voice cried out 'Her Highness Rafat Zamani Begum is about to enter.' Two *chobdarnis,* each holding a mace, walked in front of Apa Jan. Two *khwajasaras* in glittering, embroidered uniforms walked behind. It was a sight to behold. Everyone stood up and bowed to pay their court *ada'abs.*

Apa Jan looked beautiful in her diamond crown and diamond necklace. Supporting her *badla dupatta* in one hand and the sides of her *karchobi farshi pa'incha* gathered with the other, she moved forward gracefully. and took her place on the *masnad.* Bachwa Jan was waiting for the hint from Apa Jan and then she started off by singing *shadiyaana* in *raag durbari.* The rhythmic beat of the *tabla* and the sound of the musical instruments resonated in the air and rose up to the heavens; the jingling of the ankle bells rang out in rhythm and the *mirasans* picked up the notes to sing, and the *mehfil khana* resounded with silvery melody. The words of the Farsi song were:

بر تو این محفل شاہانہ مبارک باشد
الٰہی بادہ و پیمانہ مبارک باشد
بنشین بر سر تخت نازل تا بہ ابد
سرمدی دولتِ شاہانہ مبارک باشد

May this royal assembly be of good fortune,
It is our prayer that this jubilant celebration
May be of good fortune for you forever
And this royal status be yours forever.

The moment the festive song began the *nazr* started. A *zarbaft* pouch in one hand and her *farshi pyjama* gathered in the other, Darogha Kallan Sahib, stationed herself next to Apa Jan to collect all the *ashrafis* that were to be presented in *nazr*. A certain etiquette was involved. Each of the *begumaat* would bow low and perform the royal *ada'ab,* three times, from a particular distance, present the *ashrafi* on a coloured handkerchief, perform the royal *ada'ab* thrice again, then move back a few steps without turning her back on Her Highness before moving away.

Bachwa Jan now began the *kathak* dance. A silence fell upon the guests. This is a very difficult dance. The dancer stands still at first and begins by moving her neck artfully in keeping with the beat of the *tabla,* her eyebrows and eyes also moving to the accompaniment. Then the whole body, down from the shoulder, synchronizes with the rhythm of the music. The *tabla* plays the *taal* of the *thumri,* creating a joyful mood. The dance symbols describing the flirtation of Radha and Krishna are a part of the *kathak* dance and are very beautiful. Towards the end, the great dance art of the ankle bells or *ghungroos* is displayed. This is a great skill, involving complex mathematics, based on the *tora,* a rhythmic dialogue between the dancer's ankle bells and the *tabla,* until the two join together as one, into an ecstatic crescendo. The dancer has such control of the ankle bells, that they can be played all together, loud or soft, or the dancer can isolate and play just one from the entire cluster.

Both Bachwa Jan and Acchan Maharaj were the students of the famous Kalka Binda Din and were associated for a long time with the court at Rampur.

❖ ❖ ❖

MY LAST MEETING WITH APA JAN,
DELHI, MARCH 1987

Apa Jan was a very special person. She was accomplished and scholarly and had an impressive personality. When Isha'at and I went to see her in Delhi in 1986, she was unwell and very weak, but her mind was as alert as ever. She advised me about my essays, which have now formed the basis for this book and she gave me a lot of help. Then she pointed out that I hadn't written anything about our travels to Europe and England in 1932 and should do so because that was an important time in our lives, since Bahan Fakhra regained her health there.

I cannot forget the pain of losing Apa Jan. It was 16 October. The phone rang suddenly, startling me. The connection was not very clear and my heart beat anxiously. My hands were trembling. When the phone rang for the third time I heard the voice of Apa Jan's son, Mickey. 'Mummy has left us.'

The receiver slipped from my hands. The line went dead. I was in shock.

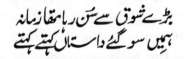

The world was listening with great interest,
It was we who fell asleep while narrating the daastan.

Rampur was plunged in sorrow. One of its greatest personages had left this world. A crowd of twenty-five thousand mourners accompanied the *janaaza*. At the time of burial the guns offered their Queen their last salute.

Apa Jan left behind a garden filled with blossoms, her children, grandchildren and great-grandchildren and they are all very dear to me.

NOTES

1. Nawab Raza Ali Khan, *Sangeet Sagar*, Rampur: Published privately.
2. Famous line of musicians in India.

A FEW WORDS ABOUT MY LIFE WITH
ISHA'AT HABIBULLAH

Departure from Lucknow

At the time of my wedding, my husband, Isha'at
Habibullah was posted in Lahore. He had a month's
leave from the Imperial Tobacco Company which he
had joined in 1938. I had been very happy in Lucknow
with his family. Mummy, my mother-in-law, and my
sisters-in-law treated me with great love and affection,
but our happy stay was coming to an end. We were
very busy attending parties and receptions nearly every
day and a constant stream of visitors kept us occupied
at home as well. During this time we went to pay our
respects to all our elders and also our dear friends,
maharajas, maharanis and taluqdars among them. I
will always remember Mrs Sarojini Naidu's friendliness
and her attractive personality. She greeted us both
with genuine affection, recognized me and said, 'Oh,
this is MacDuff's daughter.' I had met her in Delhi
before, with my father.

Our departure for Lahore drew near. A first class compartment had been reserved for us so that all the luggage could be in one place. Shabrati, Isha'at's old and trusted retainer, took care of everything. He was travelling with us and I had a *mughalani* from Rampur to accompany me. It was impossible to find a more faithful and intelligent family retainer than Shabrati. He was ready to give his life for Isha'at and had been with him since the beginning of his Company days.

At Lucknow station, all our friends and relatives came to see us off with baskets of sweets. *Imam zamins* were tied on our arms and garlands of flowers were draped around our necks. The compartment was so crowded with luggage that there were only two seats left for the two of us. In those days one took the jewellery box along too, but there was no fear or anxiety for its safety. Poor Mughalani Bua spent the whole night sitting on top of a box. Shabrati came to our compartment, at every station, to inquire if we needed anything.

Lahore Railway Station

Early in the morning, the train rolled into the grand railway station at Lahore. What a beautiful station it was, how clean the platforms! The coolies, dressed in red uniforms, waited in an orderly fashion for the train. Isha'at's friends had made all the arrangements. Accompanied by them, we left for our small, beautiful cottage, situated on Canal Bank; it was tastefully furnished and comfortable. Our friends, Syed Enver Masood and his wife, Roshan, were stationed in Lahore. Enver's mother, Ammijan was also a very dear person.

It is difficult to say enough in praise of Lahore, a city renowned all over Hindustan. Resplendent in the pages of history, it boasted grand buildings and gardens constructed by the Mughal emperors. People came from afar to admire its beauty. There were gardens everywhere, an abundance of fruit and flowers and shops filled with goods; the famous Leela Ram and Uttam sarees bedazzled the eye. British goods also abounded. The best colleges, clubs, and restaurants were to be found here. An English atmosphere prevailed in the Falettis Hotel and Lintotts. Regular events included Christmas parties, polo, racing, dinner and dance evenings; Christmas and New Year balls at the Gymkhana were special occasions. Our stay in Lahore was very enjoyable. Isha'at was very sociable and friendly and had a large circle of friends, and we were always invited to one function or another.

Muneeza's Birth at the Lady Willingdon Hospital, Lahore

There was a great deal of excitement in our house when Muneeza was born. Ammajan had arrived from Rampur with her attendant, Bunna Bua. Mummy had come with her personal maidservant from Lucknow. Every day, prayers, *nazr* and *niaz*, were held for good fortune.

The Lady Willingdon Hospital was very impressive and run by British doctors and a British-trained staff; it was spotlessly clean and the rules were so strict that Ammajan and Mummy were not allowed in the hospital while I was in labour. On the morning of 17 January 1944, Muneeza came into this world. I was overjoyed. She was a pretty baby, her features so beautiful one would think they had been etched by an artist's pen. She weighed seven pounds. The name

'Muneeza' was suggested by Mummy, which we all liked immensely; it was taken from the *Shahnama* of Firdausi:

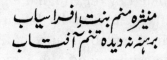

In Lahore the company manager, Charles Kindersley, announced a holiday on the day of Muneeza's birth.

From Lahore we were transferred to Jalpaiguri, a small hill town near Darjeeling. At the time the manager there was Nigel Hogg. His son, David, was Muneeza's age. We celebrated Muneeza's second birthday there. There were very few people we could socialize with in Jalpaiguri, but luckily we were not there long. We were happy to hear of our transfer to Kanpur; it was very close to Lucknow and both Enver and Roshan Masood were posted there too. We saw them every day and their daughter, Shehrazad, was the same age as Muneeza. Then we received orders that we were to move to Delhi in 1947 and from there, we would be posted to Karachi, but Pakistan had not come into being, at the time.

Partition

Before we knew it we learnt that India was to be divided and Partition came suddenly on 14 August 1947. This was the day Pakistan was established. What sacrifices had to be made, what torment was visited upon the people who were moving from one part of Hindustan to the other! May God save us from another day like that. Delhi was ablaze and there was widespread fear, panic and dread among the people. We heard that Scindia House, where we lived, was in danger, so Isha'at's brother, Enaith Habibullah, immediately took us to his bungalow which, because he was in the army, was under military protection. His wife, Hamida Bhabi, reassured us and provided us with every comfort imaginable. Their house was full of relatives and friends. She took care of everyone. I don't know how she managed to make arrangements for provisions and other necessities considering there was firing going on all around; it's difficult to fully describe her extraordinary grace and hospitality. At the time, my brother Yaqub, was on the Viceroy's staff; he would come in an armoured car, just to inquire after us.

When conditions improved somewhat we made plans to go to Rampur and Lucknow. The company had booked seats for us on the PNO liner leaving for Karachi in December. We left Bombay in the December of 1947. Although the ship was packed, we had comfortable quarters and in the commotion we ran into Ammajan's cousin, Begum Moazzam Mohammad Khan. She and her family were also on board. On the third day we glimpsed the harbour of Karachi.

We thanked God that we had arrived safely on the soil of Pakistan. Karachi was a very clean city and its cool sea breeze was very good for health. There was little greenery, but there were many coconut and banana trees. The evenings by the sea were particularly delightful with the rolling waves, the setting sun and fisherman casting their nets.

Naturally when Pakistan came into existence it faced innumerable difficulties, but such was the passion and zeal of the people that, forgetting all else, they worked diligently and tirelessly, and in a short time Pakistan was a known entity on the world map.

Since there was an acute housing shortage at this time, the Pakistan Tobacco Company made arrangements for our stay at Central Hotel. Bernard Fane-Saunders took over as chairman of the company in 1948. A far-sighted and learned person, he made it possible for the company to grow and establish itself in both East and West Pakistan. His wife, Aylish Fane-Saunders, was a very imposing lady of the old school. She showed a great interest in all the company wives and kept in close contact with them. She was very kind to me when my second child, Naushaba was born, because none of my relatives could come from India to be with me, due to Partition.

Birth of Naushaba at the Holy Family Nursing Home, Karachi

3 September 1948, was the day when Naushaba was born, just before midnight. Isha'at and I were very happy at the birth of another daughter. I had the best of care at the Holy Family Hospital. Naushaba was a very pretty baby, like a small doll, only six lbs. When Muneeza saw her the next day she was overjoyed. Mummy had chosen Naushaba's name; it was the name of Alexander the Great's wife. I couldn't get a private room in the hospital, so the doctor gave us permission to go back to the hotel on the fourth day, but a private nurse was assigned to me round the clock.

11 September was that sad day when Quaid-i-Azam, Muhammad Ali Jinnah passed away. A storm of lamentation broke loose. Quaid-i-Azam's body was being brought back from Quetta. Huge crowds gathered at the airport. A spirit of melancholy pervaded the city. In the midst of all this, no one knows why, there was disturbance in the city and a fire

broke out in the Central Hotel, which was next to the Governor-General's House. We were beside ourselves with apprehension when we heard the news. Hurriedly picking up Naushaba from her cot, we got into the car and drove to a friend's house. In the evening, when the situation was under control, we returned to the hotel and thanked God for our safety.

After the debacle at Central Hotel we were transferred to Lahore. Naushaba was two weeks old at the time. We were given a bungalow by the company and had all the comforts of home at last. In addition, the presence of relatives and friends made our life in Lahore very pleasant. Later, we returned to Karachi again and I have lived here since. Being in the Pakistan Tobacco Company was like belonging to a large family and we developed such close ties with each other, that they have continued to this day.

I am immensely proud that Pakistan Tobacco Company still holds Isha'at in such honour and that throughout his professional life he conducted himself with such honesty, dignity and a sense of commitment.

I reproduce here an extract from the tribute paid to him in the newspapers, after he died, by his dear friend, Syed Babar Ali:

'In 1947, he opted for Pakistan and played a very important role in its industrial development as one of the few professional managers at the time. In 1961, he was appointed Chairman and Managing Director of Pakistan Tobacco Company, thus becoming the first Pakistani to head a major multinational in the country. He served a term as President of the Overseas Chamber of Commerce and Industry and was Chairman of International General Insurance and of the Pakistan Advisory Board of Grindlays Bank from 1968–1983. He was on the Board of several other companies including

Pakistan Burmah Shell, Pakistan Petroleum Limited, Burshane, and Glaxo. He also lectured extensively on management techniques at various well-known institutions in Pakistan; he served a term on the Pay Commission appointed by the Government of Pakistan...He was a rare and exceptional man who loved life and lived it to the full. He had immense charm and style and a wonderful sense of humour... Above all he was a caring husband and father and a great gentleman.'

My life with Isha'at was filled with happiness and luxury and I travelled with him all over the world. I thank God that we shared so much for forty-nine years. I do regret that we couldn't celebrate our fiftieth wedding anniversary, but that was God's will. In the December of 1991 he left me. I don't know how I survived this tragedy. No doubt happy memories of the past and my children and grandchildren have sustained me and given me strength to continue. Now, I put down some of those memories on paper.

64. Bawa Arjun Singh, Kuldip Singh, Isha'at Habibullah, Nawab Muzaffar Qizilbash. Lahore, *circa* 1942.

65. Captain Sahibzada M. Yaqub Khan (later General and Foreign Minister of Pakistan).

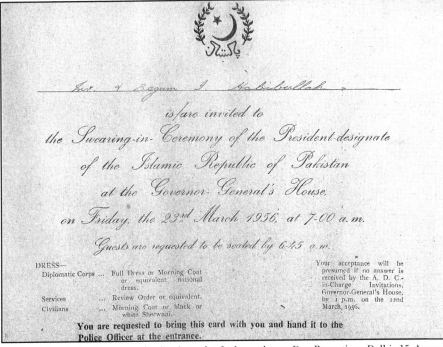

Rear Admiral Viscount Mountbatten of Burma

and

Viscountess Mountbatten of Burma

request the pleasure of

Mrs Begum Ishaat Habibullah's

Company at a Reception

on Friday, the 15th August 1947, at 10·15 p.m.

An answer is requested to the A. D. C. in-charge of Invitations.

Mr. & Begum I. Habibullah

is/are invited to

the Swearing-in-Ceremony of the President-designate

of the Islamic Republic of Pakistan

at the Governor-General's House,

on Friday, the 23rd March 1956, at 7·00 a.m.

Guests are requested to be seated by 6·45 a.m.

DRESS—
Diplomatic Corps ... Full Dress or Morning Coat
or equivalent national
dress.
Services ... Review Order or equivalent.
Civilians ... Morning Coat or black or
white Sherwani.

Your acceptance will be
presumed if no answer is
received by the A. D. C.-
in-Charge Invitations,
Governor-General's House,
by 1 p.m. on the 22nd
March, 1956.

**You are requested to bring this card with you and hand it to the
Police Officer at the entrance.**

66. Two historic invitation cards: (top) to the Independence Day Reception, Delhi, 15 August
1947; (bottom) to the swearing-in of Pakistan's first President on Republic Day, Karachi, 23
March 1956.

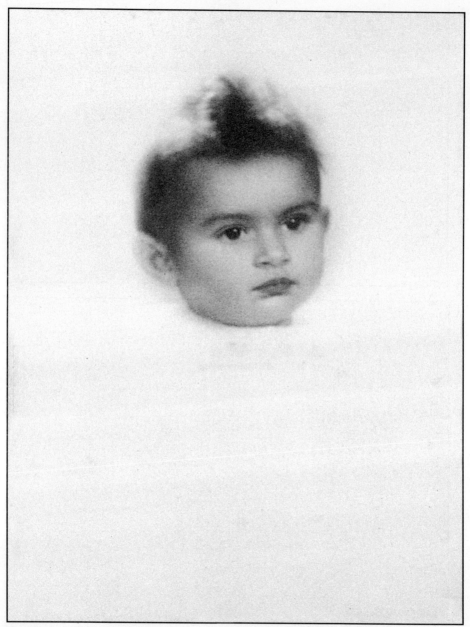

67. Muneeza.

68. Naushaba.

69. From L to R: Vijaylakshmi Pandit, Sultana Masood, Jahanara Habibullah, Karachi.

70. Demonstrating a *farshi pyjama*, Karachi.

71. From L to R: Jahanara Habibullah, Naheed Iskander Mirza, Habib Rahimtoola, President Iskander Mirza, Karachi.

72. Jahanara Habibullah with Jacqueline Kennedy, Karachi, 1962.

73. The Board of Directors, Pakistan Tobacco Company and their wives at a reception hosted by Jahanara and Isha'at Habibullah 1961. From L to R: Asma Zafar Hassan, John Astell Burt, Sultana Masood, K. Zafar Hassan, Mehru Habib, Jahanara Habibullah, R.I. Willans, Isha'at Habibullah, Elizabeth Willans, Rashid Habib, S. Akbar Masood.

74. Isha'at Habibullah, 1961, soon after he took over as Chairman of Pakistan Tobacco Company.

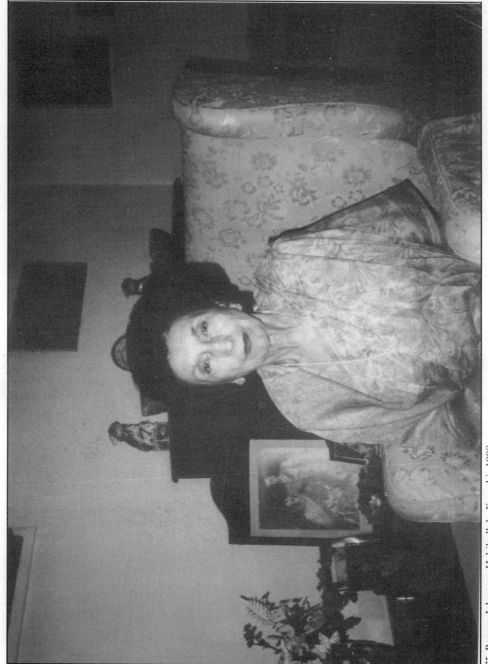

75. Begum Jahanara Habibullah, Karachi, 1998.

✣ Glossary ✣

aab-e-lehr	wavy pattern running horizontally
abba	father
achkan	see *sherwani*
ada'ab	a salaam, offering respects
adab	rules of etiquette
afsaana	a tale
afshaan	fine silver or gold glitter for makeup
Ahl-e-Sunnat	Sunni
alam	the banner of Imam Hassan and Imam Hussain, grandsons of the Prophet (PBUH)
alghoza	a pipe-like instrument
amma	mother
ankus	rod to control an elephant
ana	wet nurse
ananas	pineapple
anar	pomegranate
anchal	gold and/or silver fringe, used to decorate edges of an *orhni*

angarkha	long coat with a slight flair and with material cut in a half-moon shape covering the chest
angoor	grape
apa	a form of address for an elder sister
arsi mus'haf	the wedding ceremony during which the bride and bridegroom see each other for the first time (Persian: *Arsi* = Mirror; *Mus'haf* = Quran)
ashrafi	gold sovereign
Asna-Ashari	Shia sect (twelve Imams)
atlus	high quality satin
ba'it baazi	a literary game involving recitation of couplets
badla	golden thread used for *kamdani* and *zari* work
badley ka dupatta	dupatta in fine *kamdani* knots
bahan	sister
Banarasi	spangled silk from Benares
banat	a coloured ribbon, embroidered with *karchob*
bandhni	tie-and-dye
baraat	a wedding procession led by the bridegroom
batwa	small velvet or brocade pouch
bedanna	a glue base for make-up
been	flute
begum	lady
begumaat	plural of Begum

bela	white flower which is a variety of jasmine
bhai	brother; also a form of address for an elder brother
bhat	a ceremony, when the bride's maternal relatives present her with rice, lentils, garments, and jewellery
bhawan	mansion
Bismillah	Lit. 'In The Name of Allah' (Arabic); also the inauguration of a child's formal education
chacha	paternal uncle
chachi	aunt; specifically a paternal uncle's wife
chahgal	anklets with tiny bells worn by young girls
chaita	a purse made of *tamami*
chambeli	jasmine
chandan haar	long necklace worn by a prince
chandni	white cloth spread to cover the floor (*chand:* moon)
chanwar	a fly swat with silver handle and horsehair whisk
chaparkat	four poster canopied bed
char bait	combination of five couplets, sung to the accompaniment of a tambourine
chari	stick entwined with flowers (pl. *charioun*)
charva	a ceremony during which dry herbs, raisins and dates are carried in a silver urn (*matka*), in a

	procession for the mother of a new born
chat rang	combination of various *raags*
chattar	umbrella
chausar	a dice game played on a checked cloth
chauthi	a playful celebration, on the fourth day after a wedding
chawwal	rice
chhaiya	a *raag* danced in *tthaat kaliyaan*
chhalia	betel nut diced into small pieces
chobdarni	woman herald in the *zenana*
choga	long formal coat of rich and often, heavily embroidered material
chohel choba	moveable pavilion
choli	a tight fitting blouse
chouchak	a baby's layette sent by the child's maternal family in a procession of trumpets, a band, and singers, on the fortieth day
chu'hara	dried dates
chuna	edible lime used in the dressing of *paan*
chunree	a type of *dupatta*, starched, twisted and made up of different multi-coloured designs
churidar	tight fitting pyjamas, creased around the ankles
chutki	narrow *lachka*, starched and pinched into shell and floral shapes
dada	paternal grandfather

dadi	paternal grandmother
dalaan	verandah
danka	a large kettle-drum
darogha	palace functionary of rank, equivalent to a steward
dastaan goh	story teller
dastaan	stories of legends and myths
dastarkhan	tablecloth
deodar	a cedar tree
deohri	portico
dhanak	fine narrow lace
dhania	coriander
dhania-go'ta	a mixture of roasted almonds and coriander seeds, coconut pieces, aniseed, cardamoms and betel nuts, eaten during Muharram
dholak/dhol	oval shaped drum
dhurpad	a style of music by the sixteenth century maestro, Tansen
dullai	a light coverlet
dupatta	large scarf to cover head and shoulders
durbar	a formal audience at court, when due homage is paid to the ruler/ monarch
Eid-ul-Azha	a festival celebrated on the 10th of Zilhaj, after the annual Hajj pilgrimage
Eid-ul-Fitr	festival celebrated at the end of Ramadan

farshi pyjama or *paincha*	wide, flowing pyjama cut to resemble a long, trailing skirt; it was originally the court dress of the Begums of Oudh in the nineteenth century and was inspired by the dresses of European women.
fatwa	a religious edict by Muslim divines
Fiqah Ja'afria	Shia sect
fitra	charity on Eid-ul-Fitr
gaitli ki juti	*karchobi* shoe with a large toe piece curling back
ganga jamni	gold and silver; also term used for the culture of that region between the rivers Ganges and Jumna
ganjfa	a card game
gharana	house; dance or music tradition
gharara	an adaptation of the *farshi pyjama*, using less material
ghat	the place where washermen wash clothes
ghazal	a specific metered poem written in Urdu or Persian
ghee	clarified butter
ghungat	a *dupatta* brought forward to partially veil a bride
ghungroos	ankle bells
giloree ki go't	patchwork made of up of multicoloured triangles
giloree paan	an edible betel leaf rolled up to resemble a rose bud

girant	Stiff silk or taffeta for patchwork; similar to *qanavaiz*
go'ta garh	a man who sells *go'ta*; lacemaker
go'ta	gold or silver braids for garments etc.
godh bharai	a bridal ceremony during which dry fruits etc. are placed in the bride's lap to symbolize fertility
gokhru	same as *mukhesh*
gosh-e-feel	a sweet, crisp, flaky delicacy moulded into the shape of an elephant's ear and sprinkled with syrup
goshwaras	strings of pearls worn over the ears
gulab jamun	fried, sweet balls of *khoya*
gur	raw sugar
hakim	physician
haldi	turmeric
halwa	soft dessert with a milk and *ghee* base
Hanafi	Sunni
hansli	gold necklace with tiny bells
harmonium	musical instrument; similar to accordion in principle, but played upright on the floor
havadar	an ornate type of rickshaw, pulled by two liveried men, while a third holds a decorated umbrella
hawda	a seat for two or more, usually with a canopy, on an elephant (English: howdah)
Holi	the Hindu festival; also a style of music similar to *dhurpad*

hori	a classical style of music similar to *dhurpad*
hukkah	tobacco pipe with long tube passing through water for cooling smoke as it is drawn through (English: hookah)
huzoor	respectful form of address
imam zamin	a decorative cloth band, tied as a token of safety and stitched with money for charity
Imambara	religious building of the Shia sect
itr daan	a silver container for *itr* bottles
itr daani	a vial to hold *itr*
itr	attar; an essential scented oil
jama	robe similar to Lucknowi *angarkha*
jan	beloved, darling
janaaza	funeral procession
jayjawanthi	a musical *raag*
jhalardar	fringe
jhoola	a swing
jhoomar	jewelled ornament for the hair
jigri	tiny colourful material used to decorate garments and *dullais*
juta	shoe
kahar	unskilled domestic staff
kahari	kitchen maid
kalabattun	gold thread embroidery
kalghi	aigrette; a spray of jewelled plumes on turban
kali	narrow *lachka*, pinched to form peaks

kamdani	tiny dots embroidered densely on net, muslin, and other sheer materials
kammarband	cummerbund; *patka* draped around the waist for formal occasions
kangna	a multicoloured cord worn as a bracelet, in the centre of which is a glittering *karchob* flower
karamullah waju	God's blessings be on him (said in reference to Hazrat Ali [RA])
karchob	embroidery with gold and silver thread
katha	astringent red paste made from the bark of a tree and spread on *paan* (Eng. catechu)
kathak	classical dance of northern India
keel	jewelled stud, worn in the nose
keharwa	a joyful *kathak* dance
kemkhab	brocade, heavy silk or satin worked with gold or silver
kewra	scented extract from *kewra* plant
khaasdaan	a round silver dish with domed lid for serving betel leaves
khala	maternal aunt
khaloo	husband of maternal aunt
khatoli	small bed with small bed posts, sometimes of silver
khayal	a style of music by Amir Khusro
khazanchi	treasurer
kher taal	castanets

khichra	food offering, made of meat, wheat oats and *daals*
khidmatgar	a bearer
khilat	presents in the way of brocades and sumptuous materials, given by the monarch
khilayee	nanny or maidservant for children in the *zenana*
khwajasara	a court eunuch
kiran	silver or gold fringe
kiwam	syrup
koel	Indian cuckoo bird
koftas	meat balls
koonday	a religious ceremony at which sweets are blessed in an earthenware bowl.
kurta	shirt
la'al	red
lachka	silver or gold braid
lehnga	a long, full skirt worn by women
lehria	wavy patterns in a vertical line
ma'yun	a pre-wedding ceremony also known as *manjha*
macchi	fish; also emblem of royalty, dating back to Persian mythology
madan ban	a type of large scented *bela* flower
mahal	palace
mahalsara	private apartments of a king or nobleman
mahi maratab	high honours conferred by the Mughal emperor denoted by the

	figure of a fish with other insignia, symbolizing nobility
majlis	the gathering at which the story of Karbala is recited and retold
mala-i-marwardi	strings of pearls, presented by the monarch as ceremonial honours
malhar	songs sung during the rainy season
mammayaien	women functionaries in the *zenana*, in charge of the entrance way
mamoo	maternal uncle
mandeel	flat cap covered with *go'ta*
manjha	a pre-wedding ceremony after which the bride is secluded for several days and massaged with beautifying oils and paste
manzil	a building
maqna	a diaphanous veil of organza and gold stripes for the bride
mardana	the men's apartments
marsia	an elegy recited during Muharram; a poetic form specific to Urdu and Persian
mashallah	by the grace of God
masnad	embroidered or quilted mat for sitting
masnavi	poetry consisting of distichs corresponding to measure, each consisting of a pair of rhymes; heroic verse
maulvi	a Muslim cleric
mehfil	gathering, assemblage

mehfil khana	reception room or hall for special occasions
mehndi	henna
mela	fair or carnival
mi'laad	a religious celebration, to commemorate the Prophet (PBUH)
mia	a polite and affectionate form of address for a boy or man
minbar	pulpit
mirasan	woman singer who performs only before women
misri	clear lumps of crystallized sugar
missi	a powder for cleaning teeth and for beauty; it stains the tooth to outline it in black, which was considered very attractive
mobaf	colourful silk braid intertwined with *go'ta*, pleated with the bride's hair, into a long plait
mogra	a white flowering shrub with clusters of flowers, used for garlands
momani	aunt; specifically maternal uncle's wife
motia	double jasmine
mubarakbadi	a song of congratulations
mughalani	a superior *zenana* functionary, usually an expert in sewing, cutting (and sometimes cookery and other household skills)
Muharram	the month which marks the martyrdom of Imam Hussain, the grandson of the Prophet (PBUH) at the Battle of Karbala

mujtahid	a Muslim jurist or religious cleric.
munsarrim	a steward
munshi	a writer, tutor, secretary; also a title of respect
muquesh	a gold thread used to give a finishing touch to embroidered, *go'ta* or *lachka* work
murabba	compote
mur-murra	braid made of *lachka* or *go'ta* and made into a wavy pattern
mushaira	poetry recital
naath	musical poem, in praise of God and the Prophet (PBUH)
nagardaan	silver filigree box, shaped like a betel leaf and used for carrying betel leaves
nagni	a female serpent
naig	gift of money
namgira	an awning or canopy
nana	maternal grandfather
nani	maternal grandmother
naqara	very large drum
naqeeb	herald at *durbars* or levees
nath	fine nose ring, usually of gold.
nau lakha haar	priceless jewellery (lit: a necklace worth nine lakhs)
naubat	ceremonial music played on the drum, *shehnai*, trumpet and flute.
naubat khana	a place (usually above the palace gates) where the *naubat* is played
nawaz	maestro

nazr	an offering; also a gift of homage, usually a gold sovereign as a symbol of fealty to a prince
niaz	a religious offering of food or sweets
nichawar	money showered as a blessing or good luck upon newly-weds
nikah	the Muslim marriage contract
nizamat	governorship
noha	lamentations; poem mourning over the dead
nuqual	sugar puffs
orhni	a richly embroidered *dupatta*
paan	edible, heart shaped betel leaf
paandaan	container for *paan* and its accoutrements
pacheesi	game played with pawns, on a checked cloth
paharwalli	maidservant in attendance to a lady
pakhawaj	large size *dholak*
paraqa	border of four colours used for *ghararas* etc.
par-dada	paternal great-grandfather
par-dadi	paternal great-grandmother
par-nana	maternal great-grandfather
par-nani	maternal great-grandmother
patka	an elaborate sash tied around the waist
patta patti	colourful patchwork
peendi	large, round sweetmeats

pehchwan	small *hukkah* with long pipe, for ceremonial occasions
peshwaz	a long sleeved, Mughal dress, which is gathered at the waist and flares into a skirt
phupa	a paternal aunt's husband
phupi	paternal aunt
puggaree	type of turban
purdah	the segregation of women from men or strangers (lit: veil, curtain)
purdah nashin	a lady who observes *purdah*
puri	round flat cakes of fried flour, or layers of clotted cream
qaab	serving bowl
qaitoon	gold braid, used in uniforms
qaliya	rich meat curry with many varieties; its basic ingredients differ slightly from those in *qorma*
qanat	a gaily coloured, canvas wall
qanavaiz	stiff silk, similar to taffeta, cut for patchwork
qand	unrefined, powdered sugar
qasma	Cover for *paandan*, made of *banarsi* silk, with *paraqa* border, *kiran* and *banat*
qazi	judge or magistrate
qila	fort
qiwam	edible tobacco
qorma	see *qaliya*
raag bhairavi	a *raag* sung in the morning

raag durbari	a *raag* sung on ceremonial occasions
raag	a musical mode
raagni	the feminine aspect or mood of a *raag*
raat	night
rabab	musical instrument, similar to *sarangi*; a kind of violin
rang mahal	palace of gaiety
rang	colours
razai	coverlet stuffed with a very thin layer of cotton wool
reet ka jora	wedding clothes, presented to the bride by the bridegroom's family as a good omen
roshan chauki	kind of serenade with pipes, such as the flute and the *shehnai*, and small tambours
ru'numai	the wedding ceremony when the bride's veil is lifted to show her face to the women guests
rubai	*rubaiyat*: quatrain
rukhsati	wedding ceremony marking the departure of a bride from her parents' home
sabil	a stall alongside the road to provide water, milk and sherbet for a Muharram procession
sachak	ceremony in which the bridegroom's family presents gifts and garments to the bride on the *mehndi* day

sadra	music style, same as *dhurpad*
Saiyidani	holy women, descendants of the Prophet (PBUH), who look after the *Imambara*
salaam	salutations
salma	a fine spiral gold cord used to affix sequins
sarangi	a stringed musical instrument, played with a bow
sarod	an instrument played by plucking the strings
sawani	ceremony celebrating the rainy season
sehra	veil of flowers and/or tinsel. Worn by bride or groom; also a poem composed for the *sehrabandhini*
sehrabandhini	ceremony of tying the *sehra* to the bridegroom's forehead.
sewayyan	vermicelli
Shab-e-Baraat	a holy night when prayers are said for loved ones and the departed (similar to All Souls)
shadiyaana	music of celebration and joy
Shahadatnama	narrative recited in instalments, every day during Muharram, about the martyrdom of Imam Hussain at Karbala
shahi	royal
shaluka	a figure hugging blouse made of net or silk, with long sleeves and cuffs
shariah	the Muslim code of religious law

sheer khurma	vermicelli cooked in milk and sugar
shehnai	musical wind instrument; similar to clarion
sherwani	a long coat with high collar
shifa khana	hospital
shikar	hunt
sitar	long-necked Indian lute with moveable frets
sitara	sequins
soz	elegy
suhaag	marriage; also a bridal song—a bride's lament at leaving her parents, home
suhag pura	a basket covered with glittering paper, and containing *surma*, *afshaan*, sandalwood paste, *chambeli ka tel*, *misri*, *itr* as gifts for the bride
sura	chapter of the Quran
surma	black antimony paste, used to beautify the eyes
taal	musical tune or measure
taalab	pond
tabla	drums (always in a pair) created by Amir Khusro, by splitting the *pakhawaj* in half.
takhallus	pen-name
takht-i-haai tawafaan	a platform carried in a procession by uniformed *kahars* with musicians and singing girls performing
takht-i-roshan chauki	a platform carried in a procession by uniformed *kahars* on which

	musicians are seated and the *roshan chauki* is played
Taluqdaar	a feudal lord from Oudh; a possessor of an estate
tamami	hand-woven cloth, spun with gold thread
tarana	a form of music dating back to Amir Khusro, where the beat of the *tabla* and the *sur* of the *sitar* is verbalized (*bol*)
tasbih	prayer beads
tash badla	material spun with fine silk and gold thread
tasha	a small drum, held up with a cord around the player's neck and played with two sticks
tauq	broad jewelled necklace
tazia	replicas of the tombs of Imam Hussain and other martyrs of Karbala
teeka	a jewelled pendant worn on the forehead
thumri	a light form of music
tirwat	combination of different *raags*
topi	cap
tora	a form of *kathak* dance, consisting of a dialogue between the *tabla* and the dancer's ankle bells (*ghungroos*) until the two join into a crescendo
toraydarni	a *zenana* functionary who distributes food and sweets to the neighbours on ceremonial occasions

tthaat	root/base of a specific dance
tui	multicoloured ribbon edged with wavy *go'ta*
tukri	a patchwork of four colours in each square
turah	fan-like arrangement at the top of a turban
turunj	embroidered *karchob* paisley design on four corners of an awning .
ubtan	beautifying oatmeal paste, mixed with scented herbs turmeric, *itr*, oil of jasmine
ugaldaan	spittoon
Urdu-e-Mualla	the standard Urdu language spoken in Delhi Fort during the time of the last Mughal emperor; a collection of the letters of Ghalib
urs	annual celebrations at a shrine
ustaad	teacher (man) or maestro
ustani	teacher (woman)
wah! wah!	exclamations of praise
waliahed	heir apparent
zamburchi	small gun carried by a man sitting on a camel, during a procession
zarbaft	a superior brocade
zardozi	embroidery with gold thread
zari	gold and silver embroidery
zenana	the women's apartments